Kant's Dove
The History of Transference
in Psychoanalysis

p. 80

Kant's Dove

The History of Transference in Psychoanalysis

Aldo Carotenuto

Translated by
Joan Tambureno

Chiron Publications
Wilmette, Illinois

Originally published in 1986 as *La Colomba di Kant, Problemi del transfert e del controtransfert*. Copyright 1986, Gruppo Editoriale Fabbri, Bompiani, Sonzogno, Etas, S.p.A.

© 1991 by Chiron Publications. All rights reserved. No part of this publication may be reproduced, stored in a retrieval system, or transmitted, in any form by any means, electronic, mechanical, photocopying or otherwise, without the prior written permission of the publisher, Chiron Publications, 400 Linden Avenue, Wilmette, Illinois 60091.

Translation © 1989 by Chiron Publications.

Library of Congress Catalog Card Number: 90–1495.

Printed in the United States of America.
Book design by Ellen Scanlon.

Library of Congress Cataloging-in-Publication Data:

Carotenuto, Aldo.
    [Colomba di Kant. English]
    Kant's dove: the history of transference in psychoanalysis / Aldo
Carotenuto; translated by Joan Tambureno.
        p. cm.
    Translation of: La colomba di Kant.
    Includes bibliographical references.
    ISBN 0-933029-50-0: $14.95
    1. Transference (Psychology) 2. Countertransference (Psychology)
3. Mother and infant. 4. Jung, C. G. (Carl Gustav), 1875–1961.
5. Freud, Sigmund, 1856–1939. I. Title.
RC489.T73C3713 1991
616.89'17 — dc20   90–1495
                                                                  CIP

ISBN 0-933029-50-0

For Annalisa

Contents

Editor's note: As Carotenuto explains in the conclusion to this work, the classic analytic couple comprises a male analyst and a female patient. Because of the historical nature of this text, and because of the difficulties inherent in editing a text that frequently concerns hypothetical individuals singly, the masculine has been used here almost exclusively throughout. Overt sexism is not intended.

Preface

Two patients come to mind when I think of rapport, relationship, or transference, who were instrumental in the discovery of an area of study which up until the end of the last century had not been considered: Anna O. and Sabina Spielrein. Each of these women was simultaneously forerunner and victim in the long line of patients to whom psychoanalysis owes so much of its progress.

There are strong similarities in the experiences of the two women. For instance, both of them came into contact with physicians experimenting with new procedures for the treatment of neurosis — Breuer with the method of catharsis and Jung through the practice of psychoanalysis. Each of the two women was the first clinical case of her therapist, and both of them — Anna O. who was twenty-one years old to Breuer's forty-eight and Sabina Spielrein who was nineteen to Jung's thirty — "fell in love" with her analyst, in keeping with the paternalistic approach in vogue prior to the differentiation of countertransference. But perhaps it would be more to the point to say that, in both cases, a rapport was established between the doctor and his patient which subsequently developed into an erotic relationship.

In Breuer's case, his involvement in the relationship was such that his wife was forced to present him with an ultimatum: he must choose between her and Anna O. He opted for wife and family.

Jung found himself in an equally difficult situation. His patient, after her cure, began studying with the medical faculty at Zürich University, becoming his student, attending his lessons, and collaborating with him on the study of schizophrenia, which would be the subject of her graduate thesis. By April of 1908, their relationship had become an ardent and erotic one. Jung wrote passionate letters to Sabina (see Carotenuto 1980) describing his dream of a life "as free and independent as that of Otto Gross," which would transcend bourgeois existence. However, in his case as well, the dream faded in the wake of a wife's confrontation. Mrs. Jung appealed directly to the patient's mother. And Jung, fearing a scandal that might harm his career (he was at the time training with Bleuler), ended his relationship with Sabina in a manner that he himself, when confiding to Freud, did not hesitate to define as "a piece of knavery" (McGuire 1974, p. 236).

Both women were dangerously wounded by the relationship. Anna O. fell into such a state as to be committed to a psychiatric institution, where she remained for many years as a morphine addict, suffering prepsychotic disturbances. Sabina Spielrein's reaction was less intense and dramatic. Nevertheless, she would spend the rest of her life in a state of psychological suffering. She would be restless, unstable, unhappy. In "Destruction as a Cause of Birth" (Spielrein 1912), which was her second piece of scientific research and perhaps her most significant work, Sabina quotes Jung revealingly: "A woman who gives herself up to passion, particularly under present-day conditions of culture, experiences the destructive side only too soon" (Jung 1915, p. 116).

Both women caused the breaking off of a relationship between two researchers who had until then worked amiably together toward the same goals. Anna O. caused the rupture directly, Sabina Spielrein indirectly.

Breuer, in order to protect himself, was obliged not only to flee from Anna O., but also to end his collaboration with Freud. The official explanation given for the separation cites a professional difference of opinion of Freud's theory of infantile sexuality. However, the explanation was a cover-up for what was actually a transference experienced dramatically, in the first person. That the disagreement was simply a pretext is evident in light of the destructive violence that resulted in an enmity between them which lasted up until the death of Breuer, thirty years later.

Jung's situation was more complicated, but in his case as well, a disagreement as to concepts — once again related to the importance of sexuality — is merely a pretext, glossing over the reality of the sexual intensity he experienced in his relationship with Sabina Spielrein. Here, as in Breuer's case, the question could be asked whether or not such a difference of opinion should necessarily have resulted in such an excessive degree of animosity (see McGuire 1974, p. 27). The letter cited is proof indeed that had the same differences existed a year before the affair began, the friendship between the two men would not have been affected. The suspicion that we are dealing with mere pretext is further confirmed by the mortal blow dealt Freud by Jung in 1934 in Nazi Germany, when he defined Freud's theory on sexuality as "a morass of banal infantilism" and a "garbage bin of unrealizable infantile wishes" (Jung 1934, p. 166). An additional complication was Jung's sense of guilt—which he himself acknowledges in his letter to Freud of June 21, 1909—not only toward Sabina, whom he had abandoned in a wounded state, but also toward Freud, whom he had deceived for years (see McGuire 1974, pp. 71, 207, and 211). We might wonder whether that developed revenge was not in fact an attempt on Jung's part to work out his sense of guilt by destroying the person inspiring it.

I should like to pause at this point to consider the influence that the experiences of Anna O. and Sabina Spielrein have had on the theory and practice of psychoanalysis.

Both women were instrumental in subsequent developments in psychoanalytic treatment. Anna O. discovered the value of unguided free association and coined the terms, *talking cure* and *chimney sweeping*. She helped Breuer discover the essence of the "relationship" and the cathartic effect. Spielrein aided Freud in arriving at a better understanding of the nature of transference, in recognizing countertransference as one of the components of the psychoanalytic process and the necessity of providing an immediate remedy. Freud would find the antidote for countertransference in didactic analysis and discover the even more fundamental principle that the analyst's actions are neither objective nor objectifying as are those of a scientific observer, and that "no psychoanalyst goes further than his own complexes and internal resistance permit" (Freud 1910, p. 145). It would appear that the relationship between Jung and his patient helped Freud increase his knowledge of the psychoanalytic process, for if we trace the various phases of Spielrein's tragedy, we discover that the dates on which Freud acquired new insights regarding Sabina coincide with the dates on which he formulated concepts on new aspects of the dynamics of transference and countertransference (Cremerius 1984, pp. 3–36). Until then, Freud had seen only the effects of transference in the relationship between patient and analyst. The letter of March 7, 1909, in which Jung informs Freud that a patient (Sabina) is threatening to cause a scandal because he will not agree that she bear his child, reveals to Freud that the analyst as well can be "scorched by the love with which we operate—such are the perils of our trade" (McGuire 1974, p. 210). Freud's reply, sent to Jung three days after receiving his letter, illustrates just how strongly the theoretical problem attracted him:

> Such experiences, though painful, are necessary and hard to avoid. Without them we cannot really know life and what we are dealing with. I myself have never been taken in quite so badly, but I have come very close to it a number of times and had a narrow escape. I believe that only grim necessities weighing on my work and the fact that I was ten years older than yourself . . . have saved me from similar experiences. But no lasting harm is done. They help us to develop the thick skin we need and to dominate "countertransference," which is after all a permanent problem for us; they teach us to displace our own affects to best advantage. They are a blessing in disguise. (Ibid., pp. 230–231)

This is the first time the expression "countertransference," which subsequently became a scientific term, appears in the literature of psychoanalysis. Freud recognized immediately the enormous importance of the phenomenon, and in March of the following year, at the Second International Congress at Nuremberg, he spoke on the subject in a lecture entitled, "The Prospectives of Psychoanalytic Therapy." His lecture was published the same year on the front page of the *Zentralblatt für Psychoanalyse*:

> Other innovations in technique relate to the physician himself. We have become aware of "countertransference," which arises in him as a result of the patient's influence on his unconscious feelings, and we are almost inclined to insist that he shall recognize this countertransference in himself and overcome it. . . . We have noticed that no psycho-analyst goes further than his own complexes and internal resistences permit. (Freud 1910, p. 144)

Here, the degree of Freud's preoccupation is evident in the proposal he makes to minimize that danger:

> [A]nd we consequently require that he shall begin his activity with a self-analysis and carry it deeper while he is making his observations on his patients. Anyone who fails to produce results in a self-analysis of this kind may at once give up any idea of being able to treat patients by analysis. (Ibid., p. 145)

Two years later he states that one of the merits of the Zürich School of analysis was "that they laid increased emphasis on this requirement, and have embodied it in the demand that everyone who wishes to carry out analyses on other people shall first himself undergo analysis by someone with expert knowledge" (Freud 1912, p. 116). Who imposed this condition? Was it Jung himself after having had to deal with the consequences of his own failure? The texts do not clarify this point.

Once aware of the Jung/Spielrein case, Freud would constantly verify whether or not his students were involved in similar situations.

> Frau C. has told me all sorts of things about you and Pfister, if you can call the hints she drops "telling"; I gather that neither of you has yet acquired the necessary objectivity in your practice, that you still get involved, giving a good deal of yourselves and expecting the patient to give something in return. Permit me, speaking as the venerable old master, to say that this technique is invariably ill-advised and that it is best to remain reserved and purely receptive. . . . I believe an article on "countertransference" is sorely needed; of course we could not publish it, we should have to circulate copies among ourselves. (McGuire 1974, pp. 475–476).

Freud's desire to keep the article hidden reveals his fear of the reaction of the middle class which espoused the double standard of Victorian morality and which would have considered the fact of a doctor being sexually excited by a patient an occurrence meriting legal action.

Freud mentions countertransference one last time in 1914, and on that occasion as well the impression is that he is referring to Jung. He cites the case of an analyst who reciprocates the transference love of a patient with a "countertransference which is always there, lying in wait," a countertransference characterized by its "pride of conquest." "He must recognize," continues Freud, "that the patient's falling in love is induced by the analytic situation and is not to be attributed to the charms of his own person" (1914, pp. 160–161).

That it should have taken Freud so long to understand the relationship between Jung and Spielrein—or, more precisely, to understand Jung's involvement—is strictly due to his concept of transference as exclusively endopsychic, that is, outside the sphere of the real relationship. "These reproductions," says Freud, "which occur with such unwished-for exactitude, always have as their subject some portion of infantile sexual life, of the Oedipus Complex that is, and its derivatives" (1920, p. 18). The physician "is introduced into one of the psychical 'series' which the patient has already formed" (Freud 1912, p. 100). This idea of an automatic, nonhistorical transference led Freud to concentrate his attention exclusively on Sabina. Jung's comments on Sabina's behavior (for example, her desire to have his child) were for Freud proof that it was a question of transference and not a real love story—particularly since Jung had assured him, "I have always acted the gentleman towards her" and "I am the most innocent of spouses. . . . Such stories give me the horrors" (McGuire 1974, pp. 207, 212). Carotenuto gives the same explanation as Freud of Jung's behavior and interprets it, considering that the patient was psychotic, as a "psychotic countertransference." In this way, Jung is exonerated, and his behavior placed beyond the limits of moral judgment.

Another element, the historical one, might help us to understand a bit more. Defined, as we have seen, as an impersonal and nonhistoric phenomenon, transference was considered in the beginning by Freud to be the female patient falling in love with her male analyst. In those early years of psychoanalysis, Breuer and Freud himself, as well as other colleagues, were witness to unexpected manifestations of love by women patients. (Recall that all the patients in the clinical cases described by Freud up until 1905 were women.)

In refusing to admit the social implications of those manifestations (i.e., that the women were above all victims of a severe sexual morality and, with their hysterical symptoms, expressed what Freud called the unlived, desired, and repressed sexual life), this explanation of the phenomenon reflected the fears and fantasies of the males of that era, expressions of which can be found in the writings of Maupassant (one of Freud's favorite authors), Schnitzler, Strindberg, Wedeking, and others. "Woman" was Lulù, a dangerous creature driven by that instinct so destructive to the ordered and spiritual masculine world. In fact, Jung wrote to Freud on June 4, 1909: "She [Spielrein] was, of course, systematically planning my seduction" (McGuire 1974, p. 228). The two men shared the same concept of woman. Further, Freud wrote:

> He [the analyst] must keep firm hold of the transference-love, but treat it as something unreal . . . which must assist in bringing all that is most deeply hidden in the patient's erotic life into her consciousness and therefore under her control. (1914, p. 166)

In this early concept of transference, the analyst was the patient's victim, and once again we see countertransference conceived of as the analyst being emotionally trapped by the woman, as something "which arises in him as a result of the patient's influence on his unconscious feelings" (Freud 1910, p. 144). Jung follows the same train of thought when, in explaining his reaction to Sabina falling in love, he gives Freud three different explanations as to how, under "the patient's influence," he was captured. The first is Sabina's state of being in love in itself, the second indicates the presence of a screen or cover memory: "then the Jewess popped up in another form, in the shape of my patient" (McGuire 1974, p. 229). The third is the influence exerted by another patient Jung had in analysis at the same time as Sabina, Otto Gross. "During the whole business Gross's notions flitted about a bit too much in my head. . . . Gross and Spielrein are bitter experiences. To none of my patients have I extended so much friendship and from none have I reaped so much sorrow" (ibid.). What does Jung intend when he speaks of the ideas of Otto Gross? Otto Gross, about whom Freud wrote to Jung on February 18, 1909, declaring that Jung and Gross were the two most original among his students (Green 1976, p. 59) preached free love, polygamy, and the total and unconditional freedom of the sexual instinct. Jung wrote to Freud on September 25, 1907:

> Dr. Gross tells me that he puts a quick stop to the transference by turning people into sexual immoralists. He says the transference to the analyst and its persistent fixation are mere monogamy symbols and as such symptomatic of repression. The truly healthy state for the neurotic is sexual immorality. (McGuire 1974, p. 90)

And, although at the end of the letter he condemns such principles, a few lines earlier he states: "I envy him [referring to Eitington] his uninhibited abreaction of the polygamous instinct. I therefore retract 'impotent' as too compromising" (ibid.). In this context, compare the following passage from Sabina's letter to Freud: "He preached polygamy; his wife was supposed to have no objection, etc., etc. Now my mother receives an anonymous letter" (Carotenuto 1980, p. 93). Mrs. Jung was in fact not of the same opinion as her husband.

The basis of the analytic relationship between analyst and patient is the countertransference, that is, the permanent work of the analyst on it. It cannot and must not be eliminated — as Freud, frightened by the discovery, suggested — through the analyst's self-analysis because, as we now know, countertransference is a fundamental element in the positive progress of the analytic process. In addition, in order to avoid its becoming a destructive element, as it did in the case of Jung and Sabina Spielrein, it must be made the focal point of the analysis.

If it is true that none of us will succeed in remaining uninvolved, it is also true that we must resolve the countertransference. In this way, the patient will be able to observe in the analyst how analysis functions. We must not forget the positive effects that countertransference can have on the analytic process, or the considerable aid in diagnosing it provides as an indicator of the unconscious processes of the patient.

I have told the stories of Anna O. and Sabina Spielrein as a warning to those who do not sufficiently appreciate the dangers inherent in the analytic relationship. I have also attempted to demonstrate that in psychoanalysis, as in medicine in general, progress will claim its victims. This statement is not meant as a criticism. Such dangers must necessarily be a part of an activity such as psychoanalysis where the persons practicing it cannot isolate elements such as their own subjectivity, wherein lie the vestiges of their neuroses, the stories of their lives, their personal likes and dislikes, their unconscious prejudices. The results of the analysis of Dora showed us that even Freud did not remain unscathed.

Hopefully, the memory of the victims of psychoanalytic research will contribute by reinforcing the tendency in recent years of focusing attention above all on the countertransference. For, although it might seem paradoxical, positive results in analysis are possible only when the analyst ceases to work exclusively on the pathology "of the object." Success thus depends on the permanent work of self-analysis which progresses during the analytic process.

Johannes Cremerius

Introduction

The writing of any book is a story in itself. In a way, every book ever published implies a debt of gratitude to other books and to authors other than its own. This book is no exception. Indeed, being as I am a voracious reader, I couldn't begin to remember all my sources of inspiration. However, points of reference do exist which, as is often the case in the lives of those who write, originated in the books read in my youth. That occasional reading, like unsolved problems, continues to work away inside us, leading us imperceptibly in directions that subsequently become the secret objectives of our lives. It was at about the age of thirteen or fourteen that I happened upon a curious book entitled *Magnetism and Hypnotism* by Giulio Belfiore (1928). I did not realize at the time that I was about to acquire one of those marvelous Hoepli manuals that teach one variously how to repair a violin or penetrate the mysteries of Freudian psychoanalysis. I don't remember everything I read in that book, but I do remember perfectly my surprise at learning that some men possess a psychic force which enables them to cure illness in others. Belfiore, in that little book I still possess, more or less tells the story of psychic therapy from ancient times up until the time of Mesmer, concluding that there exists a magnetic fluid which, flowing through a diseased organism, cures illness.

I had long since forgotten that book when, while leafing through an old American psychoanalytic review of 1943, I came upon an article by De Saussure on the relationship between mesmerism and Freudian psychoanalysis. (Of course now the derivation of psychoanalysis from hypnotic practices is generally accepted, and the article might seem irrelevant.) De Saussure without mincing words maintained that in the *rapport*, a term the magnetizers used to refer to the patient/therapist relationship, lay the key to all the procedures necessary to effect a psychological cure. Personally, I have always been perplexed by the variety of existing therapeutic methods and have never been able to convince myself of any real superiority of one over

another. However, one thing of which I am convinced is the importance of the personality of the psychotherapist. This is a dangerous
enough statement to make, as all the efforts of modern science seem
to be exerted in another direction, that is, toward producing stand-
ardized instruments to be utilized by anyone wishing to do so, in
order to obtain certain irrefutable and controlled results. The justifiable suspicion is that this new dimension, in which the prevailing
becomes the method, is nothing more than noble intentions. It
remains to be seen whether or not they have been made reality.

At this point, I should like to mention two books to which I owe a
considerable debt of gratitude. The first one is Ellenberger's *The
Discovery of the Unconscious* (1970). Reading it eclipsed the Belfiore
book I had read as a boy. I read Ellenberger in 1970, and at that time
I was already familiar with some of his articles on the history of
psychoanalysis. He had, however, never before revealed or put into
perspective with such impressive documentation, certain antecedents
to the constructs of Freud and Jung. In particular he referred to
mesmerism as representing a very important chapter in the history of
Western psychotherapy, comparable to the importance later attributed to psychoanalysis. The question that comes spontaneously to
mind here—and anyone who is well intentioned cannot fail to ask
it—is, What was it that was actually operative in those practices given
that the theoretical assumptions supporting them have been proven
false?

Looking more closely, we discover with some embarrassment that
the polemics, discussions, and suggestions are identical in form and
content to the debates of modern psychoanalysis. Thus, it would
seem to me a legitimate suspicion that underlying the analogies of
form are also substantial analogies of content and that the theoretical
assumptions to which we now adhere could in future be evaluated
much as we judge magnetic fluid today. However, some common
elements remain undisputed—the two-person relationship, the psychological field, the patient/therapist relationship—and cannot, for
obvious reasons, fail to remain constant. Therefore, why not seek the
origins of the phenomena to which we have been witness during our
long years of experience only in the nonvariables?

This point of view necessarily comes up against the strong resistance to accepting the idea that the analyst's profession is based not
on transmittable elements but on events that develop within, and are

unique to, each particular relationship. The solution to this problem was suggested to me while reading De Saussure, author of an important article in 1943 on the connection between mesmerism and psychoanalysis, who in 1973 collaborated with Leon Chertok on *Freud Before Freud.* In this book he demonstrates how two important concepts in psychoanalytic therapy—transference and countertransference—were formulated in order to create analysis itself. Those concepts freed the analyst from the burden of responsibility for the reality of the relationship in the same way that the mesmerists of old freed themselves by invoking a magnetic fluid. In this book I will go into some of these aspects of the analytic relationship in an attempt to demonstrate the substantial defensive value of both transference and countertransference.

Now that I have acknowledged my debt of gratitude to books, the time has come to mention the debt I have to my patients. In our field, anything we might discuss is necessarily drawn from our clinical experience. After many years of practice in this field, I am convinced that alongside the theoretical model of the psyche there also exists a therapeutic model which in my opinion is concerned more with the analyst than with the patient. The objection could be made that this is just another way of being concerned with the patient. But, in all honesty, I must say that I have never understood how it is possible to obtain therapeutic results while maintaining a distance, that is, while denying that the psychological field created between patient and analyst is the result of a rapport. More explicitly, if the patient improves or worsens, the factor responsible is not the degree of seriousness of the illness, but the nature of the analyst/patient interaction. This is not be an easy idea to accept; as I have already said, the objectives of modern psychotherapy are generally quite different. They are suppositions in any case of ideal conditions supported by theories having no correspondence to reality. It is impossible at this point to avoid approaching the sticky problem for whose solution the Psychoanalytic Convention of 1922 actually offered a prize, namely the relationship between the practice and the theory of analysis.

I should preface this by saying that this problem is not generally grasped in its real essence; if it were, all analytic institutions would go into crisis. How many colleagues have attempted to get to the bottom of criticisms leveled against them, for example, those of the philosopher Brian A. Farrell (1981), who has been at it for about thirty years? If we examine the program of any institute concerned with the training of future analysts, it will be clear that it is structured so that the instruction of theory *precedes* any direct analytic practice. The basic assumption is that from theory definite methods of treatment can be inferred. This assumption is false to begin with; as Jung pointed out as early as 1938 (Jung 1938, pp. 565–566), one behaves in practice in a completely personal way which has nothing whatever to do with any theoretic constructs. Even the detailed technical instruments described by Fenichel (1941) or Eissler (1953) seem to be idealistic and utopian constructs without serious connection to reality (Cremerius 1985, pp. 85–98). I have often asked myself the reason for these out-and-out mystifications, for any conscientious student, after having carefully studied everything, realizes that not only are the real facts and theory far removed, they are absolutely at opposite poles. Thus, one suspects that many technical precepts are nothing more than mere theoretical appendages destined to fall apart the minute they are put to the real test. On the other hand, as Cremerius has amply demonstrated (1985, pp. 184–216), Freud was careful enough not to practice what he himself preached.

Finally, it might be wise to add that one analyst never reveals to another what his or her method actually is, but instead, lying shamefully, provides what the others wish to hear. This game goes on endlessly, seriously compromising any accumulation of knowledge which might conceivably result from a real comparison of the experiences of all. Consequently, one might ask what analysts effectively do. In my opinion, they do the exact contrary to what they say; that is, they manipulate, counsel, encourage, and promise cures, basing everything on the power of suggestion and playing on sentiments. But we should be careful about drawing any hasty conclusions because, in effect, once it has been demonstrated that interpretation and comprehension lead nowhere, it becomes clear that the emotional dimension with the myriad of affects it produces, can in reality be utilized as an explicit instrument of blackmail to correct negative behavior. The idea that patients are subjects for experimentation in order to obtain new theoretical material to the exclusion of any therapeutic ambition on the part of the analyst seems to be created purposely to justify the inevitable therapeutic failures to which slavish following of technical rules must fatally lead. And what then about one of the most fatuous statements repeated *ad nauseam* by analysts in describing their analytical experiences: "This isn't analysis, it's psychotherapy"? To begin with, this is confusing form with content. A patient laying on a couch with mute analyst seated behind, they say, is analysis! A patient speaking excitedly to the analyst with the analyst deciding to respond in a similar manner is judged anything but analytical behavior! Usually overlooked here is what the patient actually needs. I believe that, under the circumstances, only the analyst is in a position to decide that one thing is better than another. A good example of this was Freud giving money to Medard Boss when he realized that the man was going hungry in order to continue with his analysis (Cremerius 1985, p. 186).

We return here to our original discourse, that the psychological field created by the rapport of analyst and patient must remain the focal point of our research. Transference and countertransference are, as it were, the external aspects of the field which by its very nature activates experiences affecting our behavior. The particular nature of the relationship, the explicit understanding, and the various rules established at the beginning of every treatment, can bring out extremely powerful psychic images which are conditioned by a reciprocal influence of patient and analyst. Thus, we could say that we are dealing with a therapeutic symbiosis (Searles 1975). In that symbiosis, what really counts is the deciphering of this new psychic situation which, however obviously it has its roots in the past (but then what aspect of humanity does not?), has its own particular characteristics more easily attributed to the actions of the analyst than to the patient's malady. This, in practice, means that many therapeutic failures could perhaps be avoided if an effort were made to understand what is really needed at a given moment by a patient who is not well. By therapeutic symbiosis I mean the efforts made by the analytic couple to construct a model and an instrument which will function exclusively in that very particular situation. It seems natural that each analyst create his own personal mark which distinguishes him from all the others. The manner in which psychic suffering is approached reflects the analyst *as an individual*. The analyst behaves less as a scientist than as an artist for whom emotional content is the raw material of the work.

I should also like to thank all those who have stood by me through the writing of this book, in particular, my friends at the *Revista di Psicologia Analitica* (*Review of Analytical Psychology*) with whom I have enjoyed a continuous exchange of ideas and opinions for more than twenty years. We don't always agree. In fact, I could say that the very basis of our friendship is a fundamental difference of opinion, and that very often our heated discussions serve each of us simply to reinforce our own original points of view. I am also indebted to Daniela Bucelli and Anna Maria Sassone, the severest of my critics, to whom I am truly grateful.

One

The Investigation Committee Inquires

Transference is as old as psychotherapy (Ehrenwald 1976), although it has taken a long time for psychotherapists to admit the fact and finally accept it as a therapeutic instrument (Racker 1968). The danger or the temptation to place its origins back in who knows what distant time, like certain histories of the cinema which begin in the caves of Altamira, or those histories tracing comic strips back to the friezes of the Parthenon of Trajan's Column, or even those who claim Sophocles' *Oedipus Rex* or Plutarch's *Life of Coriolanus* as the original detective novel. We can sidestep this temptation, eliminate the danger, by simply adding the adjective *scientific* to the noun *psychotherapy*, because if it is true that the demand for and the practice of psychotherapy is as old as psychological maladies themselves, it is equally true that *scientific psychotherapy* originated, as did so many other sciences and parasciences, in the eighteenth century.

The French Enlightenment, the Century of Reason, was one continuous flowering of scientific disciplines, some of which, like phlogistic chemistry, the study of animal magnetism, and the study of features or physiognomy, were very new. It would seem that the dominion of reason no longer admitted confines, not even — paradoxically — between the rational and irrational. The traditional conflict over areas of authority or competence was resolved by means of an ingenuous and ingenious *escamotage*: the investigation of a mystery with the instruments of reason. Thus, alongside the study of organic chemistry and celestial mechanics were white magic and theosophy. Philosophical tracts were actually written on ghosts and specters of the dead (Tuomela 1985).

Essentially, this strategy was the only one which would permit those irresistibly attracted by the irrational to delve into it and cultivate it without transgressing the cultural imperatives of the times. As a matter of fact, this same strategy was taken out again and dusted off a century later—it was widely exploited at the very height of positivism.

It was then a question of rendering objective the entire universe, or more precisely, all possible universes. It goes without saying that so encompassing a project could not fail also to involve medicine, the discipline which interests us most because it was there that scientific psychotherapy was conceived. In fact, we will shortly see how physicians had more motivation than the other "doctors" for considering objectification a primary requisite.

When, in the last quarter of the eighteenth century, the German physician, Franz Anton Mesmer settled in Paris and opened a studio for the treatment of nervous disorders, the medical profession was divided as to the relative importance of the scientific necessity of experimental research (in such areas as pharmacology, symptomatology, and anatomical dissection, for example) and the philosophical exigency of legitimizing and raising the status of therapeutic precepts by attaching them to theoretical constructs and systems based on universal principles (Paulet 1784; De Villers 1787; Maggiorani 1880; Belfiore 1928, pp. 33–47; Zweig 1931, pp. 25–109; Servadio 1938, pp. 13–15; Marks 1947, pp. 40–57; Podmore 1963; Ehrenwald 1966, pp. 40–56; Ellenberger 1970; Vinchon 1971; Chertok and De Saussure 1973, pp. 11–20; Rausky 1977; Boille 1985).

It was an uneven match, however, because the prevailing philosophical climate increasingly tended to impose its priority. This state of affairs increased enormously the distance separating physicians coming from the universities where they had acquired a series of general principles on the origins of illness and the empiricists or practitioners who treated illness without the support of a theoretical structure.

The percentage of successful treatment appears to have been about the same for both groups. However, if the practitioner could limit himself to diligently applying his empirical remedies and, in the more exceptional cases, accept with pleasure being considered some sort of witch doctor gifted with powers mysterious even to himself, the university physician absolutely had to know *why* his patients recovered, if they recovered.

At that time, anyone choosing medicine as a profession had an additional motive for demanding an objective vision of the work. The fact is that, unlike those who concerned themselves with sulphur dioxide or comets, the physician was required to work with the most complex and alarming of creatures, his fellow man. This involved dealing with a world of sentiments, emotions, desires, and fears, all of which required an infinite amount of caution. Anything could happen, even conceivably finding oneself face to face with oneself at the risk and peril of having to call that self into question. As we know, there are those who, if faced with a similar prospective, would prefer death.

We will explore later why a vulnerable person chooses a profession that could involve jeopardizing his interior establishment. Here it will suffice to say that today, as in the late eighteenth century, this choice, together with the risks, offers solid and reassuring guarantees. Already, the prospect of dealing with organs rather than organisms allows the physician to keep a distance from the object of investigation. But the most dependable guarantee is the "scientific nature" of the contact which regulates it, sterilizes it, establishes a rigorous and functional structure, and removes the emotional charge.

Mesmer, however, treated nervous disorders, and any scientific nature in his field was still a future thing. Nothing in the general beliefs of the day even vaguely resembled a theory upon which a method for treating nervous disorders could be based. There was nothing to be done but invent one. Grafting astrology and the theory of earth and animal magnetism onto his knowledge of medicine, Mesmer hypothesized a universal fluid, a constitutive element, fundamental to humanity and all other entities, a means of connection between humanity and all the rest, including fellow human beings. Thus, illness—any illness—was nothing more than the upsetting of the balanced distribution of that fluid. Consequently, the task of the therapist was to reestablish that equilibrium by opportunely activating and directing the flow of magnetic currents.

This theory provided a logical enough explanation as to why it was that Mesmer's patients fell into a trance following the application of magnets, their state of health improving for relatively long periods of time.

Mesmer has been compared to Christopher Columbus (Ellenberger 1970, p. 57), and the simile is more apt than it might at first appear. Mesmer also stepped onto a new continent *without knowing first exactly what continent it would turn out to be*. He had had an extraordinary intuition, but in practice he converted and "patented" it within the limits imposed by contemporary concepts.

Mesmer's West Indies were earth and animal magnetism, but what he had actually glimpsed was nothing less than the transference. He had thus intuited the therapeutic value of the patient/ psychotherapist relationship. However, the necessity of bestowing scientific status on that relationship led him to seek enlightenment from the sciences of his time.

Certainly, the magnetic field resembles very little the psychological field (Lewin 1935), as we perceive it today, the most obvious difference being that, while the latter is the result of a *dual* relationship, the magnetic field invoked by Mesmer was universal. But, in this as well, Mesmer followed the contemporary mainstream: a universal field satisfied what we defined above as a primary need of the physicians of the time. In other words, it protected them from involvement in the first person in what occurred with the patient. On the sentimental and emotional level there was the willingness to admit nothing more than a vague expectation *on the part of the patient* as regards the figure of the therapist. The therapist's role thus could be compared to that of the defense attorney or public prosecutor who dons the robe at the moment of pleading a cause.

Can we be absolutely certain that this primary necessity to avoid first-person involvement was the exclusive perogative of the therapists of Mesmer's time? The moment it became eligible for the title of "science," psychotherapy assumed the obligations common to the physical sciences. In the first place, instead of limiting itself to enumerating phenomena, it attempted to organize them into systems. From that moment on, for psychotherapists, the new oath of Hippocrates included an additional clause: the obligation of assuming a metapsychology. Certainly, one could object that defining the forces evoked and utilized in the therapist/patient relationship as magnetic fluid was in the end nothing more than giving a name to something which remained as fleeting and incomprehensible in its essence and its "laws" as before. The same statement could be made regarding what we today call the libido.

It might be more to the point to say that the concept of a magnetic field, like the concept of the libido, was used for phenomena which involved more complex interaction. In fact, Mesmer could be considered the precursor of what would subsequently be called group therapy. It was in order to satisfy the increasing demand for magnetic treatment that he invented "tub therapy." The equipment he used on these occasions included

> a tub about 6–7 feet in diameter and 18 inches high. Inside a double bottom on which were placed fragments of broken bottles, sand, stones, broken sticks of sulphur and iron shavings. The tub was filled with water and then covered with slats nailed to the tub. On the surface of the cover, at a distance of 6 inches from the edge, various holes were made through which iron bars passed in such a way that one end went to the bottom of the tub and the other curved outside touching the patient's stomach or any other affected part. (Rausky 1977, p. 60)

However, what concerns us here is the dual relationship, because it is there that transference makes its appearance in the most peremptory and "scandalous" way. Ellenberger affirms that the most well-known and sensational cases documented all have as their protagonists a *female* patient and a *male* psychotherapist (Ellenberger 1970, pp. 891–892). It is an observation of fact difficult to dispute. Indeed, a large part of this book is dedicated to this particular aspect of transference, so much discussed and dramatized, both by those belonging to the profession as well as those outside it, frequently misconstrued by the latter and not infrequently by the former.

The force field generated by the meeting of patient and psychotherapist, however those forces are defined, cannot fail to be influenced by its indisputable point of departure, which is the asymmetry, the inequality of the two contracting parties, one of whom asks desperately for he knows not what, and the other of whom offers nothing less than everything, as though it were his to give.

The model of object relation which will be evoked in the patient, and to which the patient will adapt, is similar to the earliest one in his existence, that very first rapport with the mother (Greenacre 1954) — the most asymmetrical, the most disproportionate, the most unbalanced.

The term in analytical psychology for this primary relationship is *uroboros* (Neumann 1949), which corresponds to the symbolic image of a serpent devouring its own tail. The term and the corresponding image indicate the circular nature of the relationship and the total exclusion it represents for *the child* of relating to any external object other than the mother.

At the time it begins to structure its own personality, the child does not experience reality, but experiences as it were the mother (Neumann 1955, 1963). It is as if the child were not yet completely born, as if it still lived inside the mother, in a kind of psychic amnion into which the mother secretes heat and security.

On the other hand, it has been proven experimentally by R. A. Spitz (1958) that the absence of the maternal figure in this very early phase of child development — for example, in an orphanage — can cause the complex syndrome known as *marasmus*. Many psychologists maintain that even certain psychic disturbances which appear in adulthood, for example, schizophrenia, must be viewed in relation to deep affective deficiencies originating in the oral phase.

It should also be mentioned, however, that the presence of the maternal figure alone is not sufficient to guarantee the warm nucleus of security the child needs. And the very good reason for this is that — although the child–mother relationship is circular — the mother *also* exists in a larger reality from which, unlike her child, she is not separated by any sort of amniotic fluid. It is thus through her that the child can sense, for example, any disturbance or tension between the parents. In experiencing the mother, the child also experiences her anxieties, insecurities, and frustrations.

This asymmetry, this disproportion which, as we have said, characterizes the rapport of patient and psychotherapist, is increased as the reciprocal roles are reinforced. The psychotherapeutic relationship, as in any rapport involving two persons, one of whom places himself in the hands of the other, inevitably provokes a regression in one and a strengthening of the other.

It is not surprising then that in 1784 the two investigating commissions (composed of luminaries from the Academy of Sciences, the Academy of Medicine, and the Royal Society, of the caliber of Bailly, Lavoisier, and Benjamin Franklin) appointed by Louis XVI to conduct an inquiry into Mesmer's therapeutic practices, while they found no evidence of magnetic fluid, did observe a total subjugation of the patient to the therapist. It is worth noting here, although we will discuss this aspect of the problem in greater depth further on, that an additional *secret* report, addressed in the king alone, described dangers present due to the *erotic attraction* the patient felt for the magnetizer (De Saussure 1963, pp. 194–201).

Thus, the total dependence experienced in the primary relationship with the mother reappears in the therapeutic relationship, and the power formerly attributed to the maternal figure is transferred to the new figure taking over the same vital role. The image once introjected by the child is projected onto the new partner. Introjection and projection are fundamental patterns of our emotional life, and this regressive mechanism works in every contact that in some way, whether we are aware of it or not, recalls our very earliest experiences. Our expectations and our desires transform the other into the image and likeness of the figure evoked. They succeed in making us see and feel in a manner that may seem absolutely unrealistic to one who is not emotionally involved and in whom a similar mechanism has not been activated. This phenomenon is especially evident in love because in this psychological state the emotional interest is so strong it prevents us from perceiving the signals which the other sends us. Thus the interior image, unknowingly evoked, and the real image of the other are superimposed. Similarly, when we find ourselves in a state of dependence, we are induced to project onto the other all the power and charisma with which the evoked interior image is charged.

For this reason, the personality of the therapist in the analytic relationship seems infinitely superior to the patient, regardless of the real stature of the therapist.

True analysts are aware of these dynamics and know that they must adapt themselves to adjust gradually the image patients have of them, somewhat in the way a restorer reveals an original painting, removing bit by bit the accumulated layers of retouches. However, in the initial stages of analysis, this distortion is beneficial, as we have learned from past experience. In fact, the idealization of the therapist — along with the desire to be healed — was one of the fundamental factors of successful therapies in the past, the technical and theoretical content of which today make us smile (Rausky 1977, p. 198).

But going back to analytic therapy, it would be anything but beneficial for the patient should this stage of overestimating the therapist continue too long. In fact, it is only the wild analyst who, having no other therapeutic instruments at his disposal, is unable to dispense with this surreptitious authority. The inevitable result of this is that the dependence of the patient becomes more and more pronounced, to the point where the poor analyst will never be able to effect a separation. We must, of course, always keep in mind, as we will see further on, that even in the most correct of analytic situations one can never speak of a complete separation at the end of treatment.

It is very important then to remember that the original uroboros symbiosis is present in every analogous context, wherever there is a call for help, a need for nurturing. It is not unusual in an analytic relation that an out-and-out *maternage* is revived wherein a powerful figure is evoked onto which all expectations are projected. It is this projection that is the basis of the therapeutic process.

The uroboros dimension is the initial phase during which we and the universe are one. Individual identity is acquired proportionately to the extent to which we succeed in separating ourselves from the mother figure and, subsequently, the father figure. In fact, psychological growth is directly proportional to the capacity to emancipate oneself from that original dependence. Leaving that womblike state is the most difficult undertaking a human being can attempt, because the imprinting of that experience occurs in earliest infancy, during our first confrontation with reality when every event is decisive and leaves an indelible impression.

Two

Eros and the Primary Relationship

No therapist today keeps ferro- or electromagnets in the office, since it is by now common knowledge that such things are not necessary for activating a psychic "force field." I do not mean to imply that certain phenomena did not occur during Mesmer's sessions, I simply suggest that it was not the magnets that caused them. In a very complex situation, a certain event occurs repeatedly. Among the elements making up that situation, *one* is isolated whose presence is constant, and that element is elected the cause of the effect. The history of science abounds in similar misinterpretations. ➛

An exemplary case of this is the identification, toward the middle of the last century by the Hungarian physician, Ignazio Filippo Semmelweis, who worked in a Vienna hospital, of "cadaverine" as the true cause of puerperal fever (Hempel 1966; Ellenberger 1970, pp. 265–266; Céline 1952). Semmelweis—according to the version given in Céline's medical thesis—had concentrated his attention on the fact that the physicians attending the parturients were the same who minutes before "had been exploring cadavers with knives," to use Céline's astonishing prose. In other words, they had satisfied the daily requirement for the acquisition of anatomical knowledge by dissecting cadavers. Semmelweis hypothesized that those hands transmitted a substance, which he called cadaverine, that caused the mortal puerperal infection in the parturients. When doctors and students coming from the anatomy hall were obliged to disinfect their hands in basins of calcium chloride before coming into contact with the parturients, the number of cases of puerperal fever decreased appreciably, and Semmelweis considered his theory proven. In fact, cadaverine is still the name commonly given to an amine, generated by the decarboxylation of the amino acid, lysine, which is one of the products of the process of putrefaction in cadavers and also present in many other products of intestinal and other sorts of fermentation.

Certainly, the theories advanced up to that time on this subject were infinitely more fanciful: the brutality of the explorations done by students on the puerpera; the milk; purgatives; and, even earlier, cosmic, terrestrial, or hyrometric causes. But cadaverine interests us because it was the product of a "scientific" attitude or approach, part of the history of Science and not Prejudice. Here we come to the misinterpretation which is always lying in wait. If instead of prescribing the sterilizing basins, Semmelweis had simply stipulated that students and physicians coming from anatomy lessons have no contact with parturients, the results would have been far less edifying. As we now know, bacteria are everywhere, especially in a hospital environment, and the progress resulting from that intuition is now attributed to the practice of sterilizing hands and instruments of all those attending a patient, not to cadaverine.

It is true that a theoretical misunderstanding can generate practices that produce optimal results, even if later on, in the light of subsequent research and discoveries, the theory is considered inadequate. Especially in the field of dynamic psychology, the provisional and heuristic value of theoretical formulations cannot be stressed too strongly. This does not mean that it is mistaken or unwise to rely on a metapsychology in psychotherapy, only that it would be a mistake to consider it a legacy which justifies our resting on our laurels. It also means that therapeutic practice must also serve as theoretical research, not only because in this discipline it is materially impossible to separate research from therapy, but also and above all because the theoretical models inspiring us are not natural laws, but working hypotheses, or, in the words of Locke, "very doubtful conjectures," or Mach's "temporary explanations," which urgently need to be verified, revised, restructured, and sometimes even created again from scratch.

The concept of repression, for example, provided Freud with an unexceptional description of the unconscious mechanism which could have led to the formation of a phobic symptom. However, the curing of a phobic patient by a Freudian analyst cannot be considered a confirmation of that theoretical model, because it does not inform us with any certainty precisely what factor was responsible for the cure. Thus we cannot exclude the possibility that any theoretical model, provided it includes that unknown factor, could have inspired the same or other therapeutic methods producing equally positive results (Grünbaum 1984, pp. 188–189; Holmes 1972, pp. 163–170).

However, this is no reason for us to consider ourselves orphaned or rejected, the Cinderella of the professions. The philosophy of science has begun reconsidering the very concept of theory (Geymonat 1985, p. 142), not to mention truth, and even the physicists have admitted with proud humility the limits of quantum mechanics (De Broglie 1956), recognizing, for example, that in order to localize an electron, it is impossible to avoid shifting it with the very beams of radiation used in the operation. Thus it does not seem logical that dynamic psychologists should despair and feel the ground giving way beneath their feet. It was once believed that scientific progress meant an ever-increasing degree of certainty. Nowadays, we realize that often it means progressively less.

But, coming back to Mesmer, it would be wise to remember that the luminaries who conducted the inquiry into his practice and drew up the famous secret report were more aware than this Christopher Columbus of psychotherapy of what sort of territory it was upon which he had set foot, not because they denied his magnets the title of professional instrument, but because they had realized what considerable power the magnetizer had over his patients and the extent of the erotic attachment that developed during the therapy.

We know now that power is inevitable in any asymmetrical relationship, and that in the patient/psychotherapist rapport asymmetry is congenital. Therefore, for the psychoanalytic couple, the power element is established immediately upon the first contact, while the erotic attachment, by its very nature sentimental, germinates and flowers gradually, and for this reason the meeting of the two must subsequently develop into a relationship.

The erotic attachment is formed and develops in the fertile humus of a power situation. There is from the outset a *priority* of power over love, even if subsequently there is a reciprocal fueling of the two in a closely played game of interaction: the more one loves, the more one is in the power of the beloved, and the more one is the power of the other, the more tendency there is to love.

Power and erotic attachment are two pressing problems to be dealt with in the therapeutic relationship, but not equally so, at least for the therapist, for whom the more preoccupying seems to be the erotic attachment. However, it would not do any harm to give a bit of attention as well to the problem of power. We might ask, for instance, why the ones wielding the power—in this situation, psychotherapists—ever wished to put themselves in this position, since their choice, unlike that of the patient, undoubtedly was a completely deliberate one, made after much consideration, as all professional choices must be, and held to through long years of study and apprenticeship.

Mesmer, like all innovators, was obviously not concerned with such problems, but then he had seen to it that any power involved was attributed to something much larger than himself: nothing less than a universal fluid. However, this particular aspect of psychotherapy did not escape the attention of his contemporaries, the luminaries, who did not believe in the fluid. It would be very strange indeed should we, at least as skeptical as they were regarding that fluid, fail to search for the reasons that one embraces a profession whose inevitable and disturbing implications are by now only too well known.

Every choice that implies a lasting commitment—a partner in love, a profession, or pastimes which are not just fleeting interests, such as collecting or a passion for the mountains—is conditioned more by profound inner needs than by external situations or chance.

In choosing a profession, when it actually is a question of *choice*, we are guided by old, unresolved problems which we unconsciously count on confronting and finally resolving. Especially in the psychotherapy profession, we are presented with them daily, in an institutionalized and suitably camouflaged form. Even the passive acceptance of suggestions or external pressures is a kind of choice, because that acceptance is possible only to the extent that those suggestions or external impositions seem to respond to our secret needs. Even Gauguin, who worked for a few years as a stockbroker, in the end fled to Brittany and Tahiti to paint.

However, no one is going to demand evidence if we limit ourselves to stating that one does not become a psychoanalyst by chance or because of family pressure (Carotenuto 1980).

What are these "old, unresolved problems" which pop up again "institutionalized" in the psychoanalyst's professional activity? They cannot fail to be problems with connotations analogous to those which characterize the patient/therapist relationship, that is, an asymmetrical interpersonal rapport, with the power that asymmetry generates.

That problem, the most ancient one, is once again linked to the primary relationship — the rapport with the mother mentioned when describing the psychotherapeutic relationship from the patient's point of view. There is nothing strange in the fact that the same model should be evoked in the therapist, since it is the one inspiring *all* our successive relationships. What might be less obvious is that *unresolved* problems in that relationship can be referred to for the psychoanalyst as well.

This is the most likely of hypotheses (Carotenuto 1972). Anyone who has had a satisfactory primary relationship cannot fail to have drawn the gratification and inner security which permit an adult to avoid dramatizing relationships with others. Only those who experienced serious difficulty in that rapport — for example, with a depressed mother — suffer for a long time, sometimes for life, from a sort of emotional deficit which never ceases requiring indemnity. It is not a question of a vague dissatisfaction; it is an explicit demand, with two distinct characteristics — the insatiable desire to relive that experience of dissatisfaction and the need to relive it differently than in the original version, that is, in a position of power. Those who fear having the worst of it in a relationship or not being able to control it are reassured only if the other is in some way in their power.

The profession of psychoanalyst promises to satisfy both these needs. First, because it incessantly presents a rapport loaded with emotional content, and second, because that rapport is, as all therapeutic relationships are, congenitally asymmetrical. There is one additional guarantee, exclusive to the psychoanalytic relationship, and that is the knowledge that, the rapport being riddled with projections, the therapist can at any moment elude its most disturbing aspects by recalling the patient to reality, or, in other words, by separating his or her own real persona from the phantasms projected by the other. As we will see further on, it is doubtful whether this reassuring knowledge is anything more than vain illusion (Szasz 1963).

We would do well to confess here and now that the profound motivation inducing us to choose this profession is not so much the desire to concern ourselves with the needs of others as to satisfy our own.

We should also remember that the power wielded over the patient is not by the merit of the analyst, as is sometimes the case in other couple relationships, but is something given over entirely and without reservation upon the first impact. In the eyes of the patient, that meeting is truly an epiphany, the appearance of a divinity. And to gods we surrender ourselves disarmed and subdued.

The danger here is that analysts, in lending themselves to these rites, can end up seriously identifying with that divinity (Jung 1968, pp. 171–172). We all remember the impersonator of General Della Rovere in Rossellini's film who actually ended up in front of a real firing squad.

If the analyst's own analysis has not been deep enough, if work with patient is not constantly checked by comparison with colleagues, it is possible that, gradually, imperceptibly and unawares, he could experience this paradoxical reverse moral subjugation.

This deception is all the more insidious because, at least at the beginning, its effects are anything but negative. The more the therapist identifies with the projected deity, the more patient/devotees are attracted, because not only is the longing for divinity endemic in our society, it is also part of the makeup of every individual. There is a secret need in the adult to elect a new god, because the gods of infancy have been cast down from their altar. It is possible to live with the desolate conviction that the heavens are empty, but one's inner heaven cannot remain uninhabited. If parents have not been for some time either omnipotent or omniscient, if they have descended or fallen from Olympus, their ideal image is still intact and the hope alive that someone will come along to assume it.

So, if the deep motivation inducing one to choose the profession of psychotherapist is a problem having its roots in infancy, the psychoanalyst who not only accepts being taken for a god but arrives at the point of believing it, has, in order to plug a hole, opened an abyss. He has chosen the most infantile of solutions to the problem, because omnipotence, or better still the *illusion* of omnipotence, is a notoriously infantile trait.

That this legacy of infancy—like the legacy of emotional deficit— is in some way part of the complex personality of those who choose this particular profession is neither strange or worrying, unless those

14

elements prevail and the psychotherapist embraces the *Weltanschauung* of a child. His own analysis should help the future analyst to diminish the power of those elements and enable control over them instead of being controlled by them (Silverman 1985).

We say "should" because actually it is not at all impossible to cheat at this game. We might maintain that the patient never does succeed in seriously deceiving us, but in such cases we are dealing with false patients, whose only aim is to better their rank.

A personal analysis, approached sincerely, is the only instrument we have at our disposal for bringing our inner images into focus, for knowing our own Mr. Hyde, the shadow figure living within us, with which we must find a *modus vivendi*. In fact, it is not a question of crushing or canceling those images (even if, fortunately, we do not possess weapons destructive enough to do so, at least not without resorting to lobotomy) or of condemning them to life imprisonment in some sort of maximum security prison, which is, after all, what each of us has weakly attempted to do in creating an acceptable persona. It is at any rate an operation bound to fail because it causes a loss of energy, both in animating the 'shadow figure' and in keeping it at bay. ─

These figures exist, they are a part of us. If we pay no attention to them, they shout even louder or plot dark conspiracies. It would be just as well to take note of them, dealing with them realistically, mitigating their more aberrant and detrimental traits and utilizing their energizing aspects—their aggressivity—but not to the extent of certain therapists who make headlines in the newspapers when accused of violence and sexual abuse of their parents (Smith 1984, 1985). Most astonishing to the uninitiated in such cases is not so much that a therapist has behaved in such a way, but that *the patient was willing*, which is clear from the fact that it is never the patient who files the complaint, but friends or family, and that the therapist is usually exonerated by the patient who declares that she was consentient.

It is interesting to note that the "uninitiated," at least in this case, instinctively go to the heart of the problem, which is far too vast and complicated to be resolved simply by establishing the long-awaited "roll" of psychotherapists; this would just clear the way of the more scandalous improvisations and mystifications. It is a problem of vast proportions because in such episodes, besides the "beast," another protagonist is also involved; that is, the consenting victim.

The American Frank M. Ochberg defined this phenomenon, old as mankind itself, old as violence or power, as the Stockholm Syndrome, a term taking its name from a recent event, the episode of the famous robbery at the Swedish Credit Bank, during which a dramatic and unexpected upsetting of emotional reactions was observed. The syndrome consists of a positive emotional bond between hostages and their captors, together with sentiments of distrust and hostility toward the authorities on the part of the victims.

> The original Stockholm victim was a young woman who apparently had intimate relations with the robber, Olsson, in the vault, and lasting affection for him afterwards. Similar affections with or without sexual relationships have been described in kidnappings and sieges. The data available to us will not support conclusions about particular personality types who identify with captors. . . . Once aware of the feeling, it was there, more or less, for the duration of contact. Fond memories remain as long as two years, which is as long as any of my interviewees have been free after captivity. (Ochberg 1978, p. 161)

Ochberg discusses the various theories offered to explain the Stockholm Syndrome, and they all include two factors which stand out with more or less emphasis: the intensity of the experience and the dependence of the hostage on the captor.

Krafft-Ebing coined the term *masochism* in 1869, utilizing the name of the novelist Leopold von Sacher-Masoch, who, without explaining them, identified and labeled certain patterns of paradoxical behavior in which the tortured loves the torturer, responding to violence with love. The Stockholm Syndrome fits this description, even if we acknowledge that Krafft-Ebing considered masochism a perversion, one of the many which crammed his rich catalog. But even the word "perverse" can be useful if we remove the moralistic overtones and restore to it its original meaning.

We could say that any time the response to aggressivity, real or threatened, is love it is masochism. It is a paradoxical response, but not a senseless one. Those who resort to it choose unconsciously what appears to them in a particular situation to be their only salvation. If this mechanism goes back to one's earliest experiences, it can become the preferred model of emotional life, to the extent that experiencing love becomes possible only and exclusively if the same pattern is repeated.

A patient, just over thirty, intelligent, educated, attractive, and successful in her profession, recounts that she is unable to experience pleasure in sexual intercourse if she does not imagine the following:

> A man of forty attacks a young girl with the intention of raping her. He is unctuous and fat; she is slim and a virgin. The man tears off her clothes. The girl frees herself and tries to escape but does not succeed. In the end, the man penetrates her as she screams and kicks.

While imagining this sequence, the patient, who identifies with the male figure, practices autoeroticism. Only once, when she had arrived at the height of excitement, did she return to the feminine role, identifying at the moment of climax with the young girl, while her real partner became the fat man, to whom she passionately shouted, "Kill me, kill me, my love!"

Identification with the aggressor, which in this fantasy plays a determinant role, was the key to the first theory advanced by Freud to explain these mechanisms; that is, masochism is virtually a kind of reversed sadism, its mirror image, because of the identification of the subject with the loved one. Freud abandoned this notion when, in *Beyond the Pleasure Principle* (1920), he added to his metapsychology the concept of the death wish, a destructive (and self-destructive) instinct coexisting conflictually in every individual alongside Eros, the life drive. In the light of the dualistic and dialectic structure, masochistic behavior could be explained as the splitting of those two elements (usually fused in the sexual life) with the death instinct prevailing.

We are dealing here with a theoretical hypothesis and not experimental laws. To infer otherwise would be an injustice to Freud, who wrote:

> It may be asked whether and how far I am myself convinced of the truth of the hypotheses that have been set out in these pages. My answer would be that I am not convinced myself and that I do not seek to persuade other people to believe in them. Or, more precisely, that I do not know how far I believe in them. (Freud 1920, p. 59)

17

We will return to this dualistic concept later. What is interesting to note here is that, however things are, not only can it not be excluded, but it is extremely probable that a mechanism of this sort is activated in many patients during analysis. A knowledgeable and qualified analyst will not be trapped by these attitudes, but will make use of them in the therapy, helping the patient to become aware of the repetitiousness of his behavior—of the repetition compulsion, to use a Freudian term once again, although not in the accepted, orthodox sense. For Freud, in fact, the repetition compulsion, indissolubly linked as it is to the death instinct, has a tragically negative connotation.

It is understandable that Freudian pessimism—precursor and not descendant of his determinism (probably adopted more because it allowed a glimpse of the Inevitable in certain mechanisms than in the spirit of positivism)—pervades this aspect of his theoretic construct as well. We will leave to another occasion the deeper explication of these connections between metapsychology and its creator. For now, observe that, at least as regards psychotherapy, if the repetition compulsion did not exist, we would have to invent it. It is thanks to this compulsion that the patient brings into the analytic setting the living pattern of early disturbance, returning to play for us and *with* us habitual roles. In fact, the entire patient/psychotherapist relationship could be perceived as a psychodrama. Above and beyond its practical utility in analysis, the repetition compulsion possesses a positive element: it is animated by the unconscious intent to succeed finally in overcoming a familiar obstacle.

This is not a Sisyphean task, however long its history of negative results. There is an obscure need to succeed one day in dominating the anxiety a particular situation causes us, and it is that hope, even if we are not aware of it, that pushes us to search out exactly the kind of relationship and the kind of partner we do and to follow untiringly the same itinerary.

There are those who suppose that the most common method for avoiding anxiety is to avoid the situation causing it. But there are also those who correctly suspect that it is not quite that simple, who could be convinced that within avoidance lies an obscure need to harm oneself, to expiate, not having thoroughly accepted those negative results.

In analysis, unlike previous performances, awareness of this mechanism can and must be acquired. This is not just adherence to the optimistic expectations of the pioneers of psychoanalysis for whom identifying the original trauma was meant to coincide *ipso facto* with the disappearance of the symptoms, like some old detective plot in which the unmasking of the guilty party sums up the matter. The acquisition of awareness will finally permit the patient to face the problem *in its real dimension*.

Knowing what the obstacles are is not the same as overcoming them. It simply helps the patient start off on the right foot. Even after the first step is taken, there is still a very long road ahead, with no guarantees as to how far the patient will go or exactly where he will arrive. But at least it is a first step forward, a beginning, and no longer an endless, vicious circle.

Up to this point, every time our discourse on the early history of transference has touched on more recent problems, on live and current events, we have quoted Freud. This was inevitable, not only because we will never finish dealing with him — even today his discoveries are still relevant to the practice rather than the history of psychotherapy — but also because it is to Freud that we owe the first discoveries of the importance of infantile experience in the formation of the ego, that is, the structuring of the personality.

Credit goes also to Melanie Klein for having extended this area of research to include the very earliest phases of the emotional life of the infant, the lactation period — even earlier than the oedipal stage — during which many psychic disorders originate.

Among the more precocious aspects of the infantile psyche, Klein attributes particular importance to envy, not only because from it originate the earliest sensations of guilt (it is the first destructive emotion the child feels), but also because it conditions, and could compromise, the introjective mechanisms that nourish the child's ego and thus its psychic development (Klein 1957, p. 183).

Recalling once again that we are discussing psychological theories and that in psychology, as in other fields removed from the physical sciences, "simple conjectures which do not include the minimum apparatus of evidence are called 'theories'" (Popper 1963), it would be advisable to put the Kleinian concept of envy into perspective, clearing the way of equivocal false synonyms. We know that it is commonly accepted, even by certain famous dictionaries, that the noun *envy* is replaceable by a number of other nouns, such as covetousness, longing, desire, dislike, even rivalry, and above all, jealousy. Even Shakespeare, in *Othello*, does not always seem to differentiate between envy and jealousy (Klein 1957, p. 183).

It is precisely from the false synonym *jealousy* that Klein is concerned with distinguishing envy, claiming that, of the two, envy is the more precocious, "one of the most primitive and fundamental of emotions" (Segal 1964, p. 27) and giving the distinguishing characteristics of both. "Jealousy . . . aims at the possession of the loved object and the *removal of the rival*. It pertains to a *triangular relationship*. . . . Envy is a two-part relation in which the subject envies the *object* for some possession or quality. *No other* live *object* need enter into it" (ibid.).

Envy originates, paradoxically, at the time of the earliest gratifying experiences. It is the other face of gratitude, the other side of the coin. It is precisely from the satisfaction obtained from the gratifying object (the mother's feeding breast) that the desire is formed in the infant to become itself the powerful dispenser of happiness so as to be able to satisfy the need for gratification at any moment. Reality sees to it that this desire is frustrated, demonstrating that one does not possess such an extraordinary gift and that one must be resigned to depending on that object which alone enjoys the privilege. It is then that the unrealized desire to possess this quality becomes resentment towards the person who does. It becomes envy. And, as envy means suffering, the need is created to spoil the source of that suffering, the gratifying object.

In normal development, "gratitude overcomes and modifies envy. The ideal breast, introjected with love, gratification and gratitude, becomes part of the Ego" (Segal 1964, p. 39). But "feelings of envy in relation to the primary object, though weakened, always remain" (ibid.).

Why do we dwell on this theory of Klein's? For two reasons: the first is that it is relevant to our general discussion of the origins of neurosis, the second is that it is also very important in our specific discourse on transference. In fact, in the complex relationship between patient and psychotherapist, which echoes the patient's earliest experiences of rapport, this extremely precocious emotional manifestation—envy—cannot fail to be present. We will see later how it represents only one of the aspects of aggressivity the analyst inspires. Here we note that it concerns a particularly preoccupying aspect: the paradoxical mechanism generating and nourishing it — the more the envious patient asks for and obtains gratification, the more he feels his own hostility increase.

Why is it that the child envies the mother's feeding breast? Because it represents her role as originator of something which flows outward to reality — in a word, her *creativity*. The child can very well *imagine* being able, just like its mother, to produce that happiness. Indeed, this is precisely the error which continues to confound, for reality contradicts what the child imagines to be true. If it were not for this testing ground there would be no disappointment, no verification of impotence, no intolerable injustice. There would be no envy.

Satan envied God, creator *par excellence*. The creative artist inspires envy in the unsuccessful, would-be artist, who then insults him with resentful and destructive criticism. Should the creator be out of range, i.e. dead, then the destructiveness is aimed at the creation — the *Mona Lisa* instead of Leonardo, the *Pietà* instead of Michelangelo. And in the latter case, the vandal got two birds with one stone by damaging the Madonna instead of the Son.

It is clear that creativity is not the exclusive domain of the mother, the artist, and the Almighty. Our definition of creativity, the principle characteristic of which is the affecting or influencing of external reality by enriching it and modifying it, includes, if only potentially, the entire human race. One could even say that it is precisely the creative instinct which distinguishes our species from all the others.

Humanity has succeeded in asserting its presence in the world in an all-pervading manner, certainly not thanks to superior physical force or, as Shaw put it, exceptional ferocity, but thanks to the capacity to control or transform the environment. We could consider this extra instinct as another of humans' basic needs, along with hunger, thirst, sexuality, etc. Freud called it an impulse. Jung referred to it as the creative instinct (Jung 1960, p. 118). Personally, I suspect that it is the repression (once again borrowing a Freudian concept and model) of that basic need which could be the cause of neurosis (Carotenuto 1983).

Freud attributed the origin of psychic maladies to the repression of sexuality before he introduced the death wish into his theoretic construct. And he consistently attributed creative energy in all its expressions, including artistic genius, to its sublimation.

21

On this primacy of sexuality so much has been said and written, and so many schisms, repudiations, and crusades have resulted, that it would be virtually impossible to take up the subject again without repeating what has already been stated, contested, confirmed, or confuted. So we will limit ourselves simply to warning whoever approaches this *vexata quaestio* for the first time of the most obvious temptation, which is that of considering as proof the impressive number of cases of sexual disturbance treated in psychotherapy. Even if all patients in therapy had sexual problems and every one of them had come to the therapist for help because they had been alarmed by some disturbance in the sexual sphere, we could only deduce that human sexuality is so complex and sensitive a mechanism that it goes into a state of crisis at the first sign of psychic disorder. Anything else would be blaming the short circuit on the fuse, or the empty gas tank on the dashboard warning light.

For once, there is no need to cite the classic misunderstanding, *post hoc, ergo propter hoc*, because when dealing with illness or symptoms, not only is *propter* arbitrary, but also *post*. A simple diagnosis is not sufficient to distinguish the causes and effects of an ailment.

As to artistic creation as a sublimation of sexual energy, we will simply note that all the pages of this book would not suffice to list the artists (musicians, poets, novelists, painters, choreographers, film directors, etc.) who have enjoyed an intense, even excessive, sexual life.

Now that we understand the importance of Klein's hypothesis of precocious envy to our general discussion on the origins of neurosis, we shall proceed to its significance for the phenomenon of transference.

If the deep underlying cause of the malaise or symptoms inducing patients to place themselves in analysis is the repression of creativity, the psychotherapist will find himself having to deal with individuals who submit to reality because they have given up attempting to shape it to their own requirements. The patient is aware of this anomaly; however, instead of assuming the responsibility for it, he attributes it to others, which is a continuous distortion of reality, a harmful self-deception.

The first task of the therapist will necessarily be to do the best to make the patient aware of this nonlife, this mode of being lived (or experienced) by others. However, it is inevitable that one of the results of the patient being made aware of this aberrant way of being (or nonbeing) will be the conception of the psychotherapist as one who acts upon others, as one who possesses precisely that capacity which the patient does not. And it is at this point, in the patient's spectrum of reactions, that envy appears.

Effectively, the analyst *is* creative, in the sense of having decided to be concerned with others, that is, to modify external reality. Such is the case even if the therapist denies it, refuses to believe it, or insists (in excessive or illegitimate self-defense) that anything occurring in the therapeutic setting is produced exclusively by the patient. Therapists are creative from the moment that a psychological field is created between themselves and their patients which cannot be traced back exclusively to the interior life of either, precisely because it also includes the other, and thus includes reality.

Naturally, the analyst knows that envy will remain, in the best of hypotheses, an unproductive emotion if it is not directed and utilized for the purposes of therapy. Once the patient becomes aware of nonliving, he must be helped to break the intolerable regime imposed upon himself. Otherwise, he will remain prisoner in that vicious circle which he has never left.

To venture out of that circle is no mean feat, and above all not painless. It will cause the patient much suffering and part of that suffering will be converted into hostility towards the therapist who, instead of having made the patient's life easier, has placed him in peril. This is why envy is only *one* of the components of the aggressivity the psychotherapist attracts.

Leaving that circle causes suffering because the repression of creativity had a defensive function — it was adopted originally as a protection against fear, to avoid provoking the Father/Judge and all his successive incarnations. It may have been maintained thanks to the fact that society does not seem to have much need for creative individuals. In fact, cultural pressures, independent of any political bias, tend to substitute the imitation of a model for the pursuit of a valid, individual way of dealing with reality. It is not so surprising then that we talk about a creative *instinct*; it is not the only instinct that culture asks us to sacrifice.

If it is true that the patient has gone into analysis because the repression of creativity is no longer effective, the defensive role it played already undermined, and renunciation either no longer sufficient to keep anxiety at bay, or else requiring too much energy, it is also true that the new road which the psychotherapist indicates is not lacking in obstacles, traps, or difficult and painful choices to be made.

The classic example of this is seen in the relationship of the couple. If the patient brings into the therapeutic setting an inauthentic marital situation (an extremely frequent occurrence, since the choice of partner was surely conditioned by false needs, which cannot fail to surface as such as the treatment progresses), the psychotherapist will naturally avoid bringing up the problem. It will be the patient who experiences the new and pressing need to clarify and take account of the inconsistencies or inadequacies of that situation and draw the obvious conclusions.

On the other hand, in psychotherapy the patient's progress can be evaluated solely on the basis of behavior in reality. Our psyche is not an engine that can be tested experimentally. The resistances, performances, and shock waves of reality cannot be simulated in a controlled wind tunnel, as they can for aircraft. For the ego, the only reliable test is actual flight.

Three

A Circular Seduction

Immediately following personal success with patients, a psycho-therapist's greatest aspiration is to proselytize and found a school. And as Mesmer certainly was not averse to surrounding himself with disciple/apostles to spread his Word, from this point of view he could be considered the father of psychotherapy.

Mesmerism was just the first of the many "isms" which seem to make up the history of psychotherapy, one of the few disciplines in which the individual originators of ideas never become prominent unless they establish a school or current of thought, with a structure sometimes not all that different from a church or sect, with hierarchy, sacred texts, and rites of initiation.

In France, Mesmer's devoted followers were organized into proper secret societies, the Societies of Harmony (Ellenberger 1970, pp. 32–33; Vinchon 1971, pp. 105–127), which were associated in a sort of Freemasonry. But in order that the modern-day appellation "school" not sound excessively malicious, I hasten to add that there were more than just secret lodges for the adherents of mesmerism. In Germany and England, where proclamations of His Majesty, the King of France, did not warrant legal enforcement, Mesmer's theories were preached and practiced in the full light of day. Lafayette took it upon himself — or was given the task by Mesmer — to carry the new Word across the Atlantic to the United States (Fuller 1982), where directly or indirectly Christian Science, an upswing in spiritism, and a couple of the early novels of Edgar Allen Poe (1844–1845) resulted.

It was Mesmer's more important theoretical concepts, which today we would call his metapsychology, rather than his therapeutic meth-ods, that crossed frontiers and spanned oceans. The magnets and the tubs did not last very long; the magnetic fluid remained in circulation for more than a century. Even today, the phrase "a magnetic personality" is still in use, even if the reference to magnets has become a mere metaphor whose origin has been forgotten.

In fact, in their practice it was to the magnetic personality, or rather the personality of the magnetizer, that Mesmer's disciples shifted the emphasis. This could have been viewed as a step backwards given the imperatives of the century of enlightenment for scientific research (attention to empirical data, objectification of phenomena, primacy of the technical instrument), but in the evolution of psychotherapy it was a decisive step forward.

In all truth, the first "mesmerian" to effect this change in course limited himself to theorizing on the decisive contribution *of the patient* in the process of "magnetization." But we need only decipher exactly what this contribution consisted of in order to appreciate its significance. In fact, affirming that the determining factor in the positive outcome of the fluid's application was *the will of the magnetized to be magnetized* implied the direct and personal involvement of the therapist in the therapy, even if it does not actually ascribe to the therapist the mysterious healing power that Mesmer had attributed to the magnets. This is not the usual case of a patient entrusting some part of his body to a physician and his equipment, but instead renouncing his own awareness and will in order to accommodate the awareness and will of another.

The reference here is to Abbot Faria, who actually did exist, and not only in the pages of *The Count of Montecristo* (Chertok and De Saussure 1973; Ellenberger 1970, p. 75; Podmore 1963, pp. 87). José Custòdio Faria, who was Dumas's inspiration for the main character of his book, was ordained in Rome and studied magnetism in Paris, although he claimed to have had previous experience as a healer in his own country, coincidentally, the then-Portuguese India. We could wax ironic about this abbot/guru, but it would be difficult to deny him the credit he is due for having glimpsed, without actually having defined it, the mechanism of regression concealed in the unconditional surrender of the patient to the psychotherapist. It is one thing to speak about the will to be cured, about psychological elements such as expectation, hope, faith, and the conviction that one will recover, which perhaps explain the miracles at Lourdes, in short, a placebo effect. It is still another thing to speak of the will to submit oneself to the therapist.

Today we know that it is actually a regression to the infantile level which leads the patient to conceive of the analyst as so powerful and overwhelming a figure, one capable of taking the patient's destiny in hand and restoring him to life.

We also know that this is a positive process, because what the analyst will attempt to transmit to the patient so anxious to receive is not—always provided that he remembers he is an analyst and not a guru—ideological structures or contents (Viederman 1976), but strength and energy which the patient will then utilize for his own ends, his own real needs, his own projects.

That this regression is positive can be observed in the fact that it is the most difficult patients—those who discuss and rationalize and reappraise everything that occurs in the therapeutic setting, confusing their own resistances with a legitimate need for clarity—who obstinately refuse to regress. These patients are convinced that they are defending their own autonomy and intelligence, while it is actually their neuroses they are defending. In what Freud referred to as a game of chess between analyst and patient, the real adversary of the therapist is not the patient but his neurosis, which unbeknownst to him guides his moves.

We might ask how it is that a patient who, by beginning analysis, has decided to conquer his neurosis, and then allows himself to be guided by that neurosis, at least at the beginning of the game, doing his utmost best to checkmate the analyst, as if the analyst were his adversary. The explanation for this lies precisely in that infantile regression, which is inevitable at the beginning of the analysis, because it is in the vision of earliest childhood that the powerful savior-figure projected onto the analyst soon enough summons up an equally powerful persecutor-figure.

Typical of our primitive rapport with reality is the inability to accept in the other the contradictory aspects that are inevitably a part of every human being and the insistence on separating those aspects into two distinct entities, one adorable and the other frightening. It is impossible in this condition to accept another person with all his contrasting lights and shadows, because one is either fearing or adoring and always expecting that some unmistakable sign or signal will cause the opposite figure to emerge.

Many of us, even as adults, follow that old, familiar script when, as often happens in love, we let slip revealing phrases like, "I should never have expected that from you," or "I don't know you anymore," or literally, "You are not the same person I fell in love with," "You are another person," and so on into the night.

But for those patients—defined as the most difficult—whom the defense is expressed in the refusal to regress, more often than not the perfect weapon and sometimes the winning move is another. It is *seduction* (Baudrillard 1979; Rondinone 1985).

Seduce the potential aggressor in order to neutralize his aggressivity—the oldest of strategies in the history of humanity, as well as of every individual. And every one of us has at some time in early infancy felt the need to defend ourselves from the real or imagined hostility of adults, particularly parents, using the weapon of seduction. However, nature has seen to it that not only does the child appear defenseless (which for certain adults would not be a deterrent, and for others would actually function as a provocation), but it above all inspires tenderness—that affectionate sentiment which even semantically is the exact opposite of harshness and the most reassuring for so fragile a creature as a child.

To question whether it is the child who is programmed to inspire tenderness in adults, or the adult who is programmed to feel tenderness before certain inevitable characteristics of the emerging person, would be similar to asking which came first, the chicken or the egg. What is certain is that the child learns very early in life how to play its hand (smiles, mannerisms, stuttering, and baby talk) and knows that even without resorting to winning repertoire, even in sleep, it can count on the tender seduction of its physical appearance alone.

In any case, it is not only human offspring whose survival depends on the arm of seduction. Ethology teaches us that in a world where the weak or maladjusted individual cannot fail to succumb, no whelp of any species would survive if a mechanism were not activated inhibiting the aggressivity in the adult—especially the parents—because the adult of many species of mammal and even more of birds would not be disinclined to partake of such a tempting and easy prey, if some mechanism were not set off inside them in the place of appetite: the providential tenderness (Lorenz 1963).

The ethologists have explained that at least in the animal world, the so-called maternal instinct must be aroused, and kept aroused, by certain signals. A deaf turkey, not hearing the cheeping of its off-spring, instead of nourishing them would devour them because evidently that is the only signal which induces it to feed rather than feed upon. In any case, the tender ungainliness of the young has succeeded in saving various species from total extinction; every now and then the most dreaded hunter produced by nature—the human—spares some specimen because he has been seduced by its winning innocence and is tempted to take it home and raise it.

Coming back to humanity, I might add that, in this species, the adult also occasionally repeats this infantile seduction by playing the part of the "puppy," regressing when in love (romping or behaving in a childish way with the partner, mimicking the vocal expressions of a child, baby talking), even reviving the language of that far-off period of life (the "pennies," the "pappa," the "poopy," the "caca"), the way—incidentally—patients not infrequently do in analysis.

In the very first pages of the eventful story which is the history of psychotherapy, playing very prominent roles, exactly as they would in a nineteenth-century romance novel, are an abbott and a marquis.

We have already mentioned the abbot. He was the Reverend Father José Custòdio Faria, one of Mesmer's disciples, champion of the primacy of the will of the patient in magnetic therapy. The marquis was Puységur, another of Mesmer's pupils, who advocated instead the primacy of the therapist's will (Marks 1947, pp. 58ff; Podmore 1963, pp. 71–80; Ellenberger 1970, pp. 70–74; Chertok and De Saussure 1973; Rausky 1977, pp. 167ff). Two complementary wills thus lay claim to the role of therapeutic factor, with the result that the famous fluid had to be reevaluated.

There were actually three Puységurs, brothers, all men of arms like their illustrious ancestors, and all enthusiastic adherents of magnetism. But the title of marquis was the exclusive privilege of the eldest and it is he alone who is remembered in the history of psychotherapy.

Armand-Marie-Jacques de Chastenet, Marquis of Puységur and high-ranking officer in the artillery, introduced a change in magnetic therapy when instead of obtaining the usual convulsions he transported his patient into a particular state of sleep during which the magnetized spoke of his disturbances, clearly pronouncing diagnosis and prognosis (nothing of which was remembered once awake). That sleep was nothing more (or less) than the hypnotic state, although it would be many years before Braid coined the term hypnosis. Puysé-gur referred to it as induced somnambulism. His great discovery, however, was the simple but revolutionary theoretical conclusion he drew from those amazing occurrences: that it was his will to cure the patients which acted upon them, causing in them those manifestations.

> I believe in the existence within myself of a power.
> From this belief derives my will to exert it.
> The entire doctrine of Animal Magnetism is contained in the two words:
> *Believe* and *want*.
> I *believe* that I have the power to set into action the vital principle of my fellow-men; I *want* to make use of it; this is all my science and all my means.
> *Believe* and *want*, Sirs, and you will do as much as I.
> (Ellenberger 1970, p. 72)

With this pentalogue, pronounced in 1785 during a Congress of the Freemasons of Strasburg, Puységur deprived the future psycho-therapist of any hope of not dirtying his hands in the relationship with the patient by attributing to the therapy not only the contribu-tion of his individual human qualities, but also the will to invest them in the therapeutic relationship, thus assuming personally the entire responsibility.

Puységur also alerted his followers to the dangers presented by a total devotion or submission in the patient and was the first to approach the problem of the power with which the psychotherapist finds himself invested in terms still valid today, that is, from an ethical and not purely deontological point of view.

In other words, following the early intuitions of Abbot Faria, the circular nature of the psychotherapeutic relationship began to emerge as an interpersonal system characterized by the continuous interac-tion of two wills.

A clever reader might object that today opinion is divided on the therapist's Puységurian "will to heal." And this objection is not with-out foundation. We might even say in all honesty that, from Freud on, the will to heal has become progressively less popular among psychotherapists, especially psychoanalysts, to the extent that the opposite position, an absence of the will to heal, which appeared paradoxical when preached by Freud because it contradicted traditional medical deontology, but now has become almost commonplace, a platitude.

Freud stated that it was precisely that "therapeutic intent" which eliminated the minimum of scientific approach possible in an interpersonal rapport (Sterba 1978). From then on, in psychoanalysis, the point of view that therapy is an evolutionary process of the patient has gained more and more acceptance, and in this process the will of the analyst would represent a serious interference. Further, if the analytic process is to be a *cognitive* process, it is inevitable that, above and beyond the ethical question, such interference would compromise correct observation.

However, the suspicion is justified that the patient's will to heal (which no deontology will convince him to renounce) is also a disturbance in the cognitive process. Thus, going from one paradox to another, we have arrived at the same conclusion the Americans did who, after an investigation of psychotherapeutic cures (Kernberg 1972), stated that the only ideal patient is one well enough not to need a psychotherapist.

Let us see now whether it is possible, by starting from a more acceptable premise, to avoid coming to such a drastic and comical conclusion, and also to prevent the arrival of the day when the patient demands a fee for services rendered to us as incurable scopophiliacs of the psyche.

We could, for example, attempt to go thoroughly into the differences between the will to heal of the patient and that of the therapist, beyond observing the grammatical difference between the verb "to heal" which is intransitive for the patient, while for the therapist it is transitive — it takes an object. We have learned from experience that the patient, when asking to *be healed*, desires only to be liberated from something which causes suffering or renders life difficult. It is that something — symptom or syndrome — which induces him to go to a psychotherapist for help.

What then can the psychotherapist prescribe? The removal of the something as if it were a tooth or an inflamed appendix? An unequivocal response here is not possible because we must first distinguish between psychoanalysis and the various schools which concentrate on the symptom, for example, behaviorist psychology. In this type of therapy the patient who is suffering from a phobia is made to confront anxiety-provoking stimuli for a certain number of sessions. A deconditioning can result (or be brought about), thanks to which the case is resolved. The symptom disappears, but not the illness, which sooner or later reappears in some other form.

However, in this case, what is involved is not the will to heal but the decision to heal the symptom. Of course, the symptom is misleading as regards the deeper disturbance, given the fact that the symptom most probably only represents the attempt, even if an awkward one, to defend oneself from the suffering which deep disturbance causes—somewhat akin to removing the tortoise's heavy shell in order to facilitate more rapid movement. But metaphor aside, there is a serious danger that behaviorist therapy, for example, of an agoraphobe could consist simply of turning him out again into the spaces he fears.

The psychoanalyst is equipped to avoid falling into this trap, even without attenuating the desire to heal. Regardless of what the patient actually asks, we know that what is really meant is "free me from my ills," and not "free me from my symptoms." The question to ask ourselves has already been set down by our choice and the deep underlying motivations for making it.

We can speculate as much as we like on the ideal psychotherapist— a special model for technical operations in a pure state at 0° temperature, in the absence of gravity. However, if some prototype is actually in circulation somewhere, it would probably be best suited to the above-mentioned model of patient: the one who does not need treatment.

Practically speaking, as long as patients come to us for help instead of turning to a computer, it will remain difficult for us to remove not so much the will as the need to respond, in our own individual way, to that request.

Probably, in the expression "will to heal," what causes more perplexity is the verb to heal than the substantive will (with its vague echoes of Superman), because that verb powerfully evokes the figure of the healer, in the thaumaturgical, miraculous sense, and although this certainly would not have displeased either Puységur or Mesmer, or Abbot Faria—as it does not displease certain modern incarnations of the Abbot—it is rightly repugnant to the majority of our colleagues today.

Doubtless the verb to heal, particularly for those who have adopted the Jungian lexicon (and perhaps something more), is no longer a satisfactory definition of a process that is never completely terminated. But in the same vein we should also have to stop referring to psychotherapy, which, as Freud preached, far from excluding the therapeutic intent, legitimizes and institutionalizes it, differentiating the psychotherapist from the simple student of psychic phenomena.

It is not with words that we succeed in banishing the Abbot Farias who discredit our profession, any more than we can solve the problems of the blind by renaming them the nonseeing, or resolve our difficult relation to death by deciding one fine day to call the dead the nonliving.

The fact is that today, whether or not it convinces us on the theoretical level, psychotherapy exists, and its work, declared or not, has an aim, a precise intent. This means that its efforts can scarcely be directed toward the abolition of therapeutic intent, but rather at the most toward putting it aside for the moment, a tacit, implied mental reserve. A soft distant light, not a blinding one up close which prevents our seeing exactly just where it originates; or the ground bass which accompanies, without dominating, the single movements of a contrapuntal composition — this, in psychotherapy, is succeeding in understanding the patient, entering into his suffering, and finding together the way of overcoming it.

It is a question then of avoiding the *furor sanandi*, and not the faith and hope, in ourselves as well as in the patient. Because in the end the point is just this — we can impose nothing upon ourselves and forbid ourselves nothing without doing the same to the patient, just as we can ask nothing of the patient that we do not expect from ourselves.

When we speak of a circular rapport, we mean something more than a simple interplay of causes and effects. We mean a secret symmetry that emerges from the very beginning of the relationship, a promising if vague harmony that, unlike love at first sight, which can result from misleading signals, has a real and plausible basis — at least for the more "expert" of the two, the analyst, because it consists of content, even if barely intuited, and not outward appearances.

If the two members of the analytic couple do not have psychic themes in common, the therapeutic alliance will be very brief and

labored (Jung 1946, pp. 176–177). When the problem brought to us
by the patient strikes no chord within us, it would be foolhardy to
hope that the syntony will come later, as was once said of love in
certain arranged marriages. Every psychotherapist must be aware of
this, and personally, I believe that all psychoanalysts are, even if they
are considerably reluctant to state it explicitly and theorize about it.
But this reticence is understandable: a concept of this sort threatens
to reduce even further the already meager degree of science our
discipline seems to need in order to obtain credibility.

Actually, if it is true—as affirmed by the more rigorous
epistemologies—that no cognitive rapport can ever be totally free of
subjectivity for the simple reason that it is a relation between an
object and a subject, it would be absurd to think that it should be
only our discipline to escape this. We might as well make a strong
point of this weakness, using it like a precious instrument, all the
more efficient the more concentrated its use. The subjective approach
will not provide us with a master key to open any door; it will simply
make it possible for us to know after the first try whether or not we
possess the right key for a particular lock.

Four

Science for Neutrality

The circular nature of the magnetizer's relationship with the magnetized is clearly confirmed by an apparently secondary aspect of Puységur's experiments: the exchange of "deep" messages between therapist and patient. In fact, not limited to merely *receiving* what the patient, in that "state of grace," succeeded in reading in himself, the magnetizer in turn transmitted to the patient his own interior condition, also drawn from the most secret depths of his own being.

At that time the term "the unconscious" was not known, but it is evident that in induced somnambulism it was this unconscious psychism which was powerfully called up. The magnetizer as well, by putting himself into the receptive frame of mind required by that particular kind of message, or in other words, by tuning in to that wavelength, summoned up a hidden part of his own psychic life.

The psychic dynamics which would later be called transference and countertransference developed from this inevitable and indispensable phenomenon of syntonia. And it was perhaps even unnecessary that separate terms be coined; transference of the patient and transference of the therapist would have sufficed (Hoffer 1956, p. 378; Fleiss 1953, pp. 268–284; Stern 1924, pp. 166–174). As we will see, if the concept of transference met with considerable resistance from the "authorities," the resistance in the same quarters was even greater to its complementary phenomenon (Racker 1968), which not only involved the psychotherapist directly as protagonist, but even further, riveted him to the reality of the transference, his affective response, giving form to that shadow, that phantasm, that projection, in some way confirming its validity and authenticity. Something had to be conceded in the wake of such resistance — the minimum concession; different terms to describe the transference of patient and analyst.

There actually is a factor distinguishing countertransference from transference — the awareness in the former of the projective and subjective implications of the feelings activated toward the other in the unique situation created within the psychotherapeutic relationship. This distinguishing factor remains in spite of the fact that today most of those going into therapy are more or less aware of what they are letting themselves in for. Doubtless the analyst's theoretical and clinical experience, which implies an inexorable alternating of partners, compels him to view the situation from within as well as from without and consequently to maintain a close hold on that awareness.

It is important to remember that an awareness of the projective dynamics activated in the psychotherapeutic relationship in no way compromises the validity and authenticity either of the transference or the countertransference, and the good reason for this is that these particular dynamics are *always* a part of all emotional relationships, affecting the way we experience them and determining whether we accept or reject them, obviously without canceling their validity or authenticity. The only difference is that in the analytical relationship these dynamics are not lived, but focused upon and analyzed.

Later, when we go more deeply into the concept of transference, we will understand better how the symmetry between the dynamics activated in the patient and those activated in the analyst is not fortuitous but originates in the deep motivation that led the patient to go into analysis and the analyst to choose this profession. For now let us simply say that these motivations, however they may vary, gravitate around the ego–Self axis, that alimentary canal which connects the ego to the introjected figure of the parents, in particular the more protective, reassuring, and nourishing of the two, the mother. This axis *should* provide an uninterrupted flow of psychic energy. However, if in earliest infancy, at the point where the mother–child symbiosis ends and the ego begins to form, introjecting the mother figure and putting this canal into operation, some deficiency or frustration compromises the success of this delicate and complex process, what results could be called a breakdown in the ego–Self axis (Edinger 1960). A breakdown of this kind leads the patient to go into analysis, and a similar breakdown gives the analyst the capacity and the need to concern himself with these problems.

This continuous harking back to the earliest phases of our psychic existence plunges those who see analysis as an incessant evocation of the distant past into the most extreme discomfort, since the pertinant events belong to a personal prehistory which no one remembers. Actually, what is important for the analyst is not so much the patient's past as those vestiges of it that remain and unknowingly condition behavior. It is precisely from behavior that the psychoanalyst draws a large part of the needed information.

If, for example, a patient brings to every session roses for the psychoanalyst, the analyst will certainly not be content with an explanation that seemingly negates the value of the gesture ("I am always forced to stop at a traffic light where there is a boy selling roses so persistently that the only way to be free of him is to buy some"). Instead the analyst will read between the lines of this behavior, silently, to himself. In other words, he will not be in any hurry to confront the patient with an interpretation which he is not yet ready to accept.

However, the subject will eventually come up. The analyst knows very well that it is unavoidable. And, in any case, discussing emotion is his destiny by choice for, as we have already said, embracing one type of work over another is always the response to a deep need, an old problem of relating not yet resolved.

For the analyst, the unresolved relationship is with the maternal figure which he — not unlike his patient — in a sort of repetition compulsion recreates for himself in every therapeutic relationship.

In the new version of that old relationship the analyst plays an ambiguous role, at the same time mother and son to the patient, nourishing and being nourished by the pleasure experienced in nourishing. The craving for this pleasure, the analyst's need to nourish, is no less pressing or urgent than the patient's need for nourishment. Further, at the risk of too much word play, if the patient's dependence on the analyst becomes an addiction, in the sense usually associated with drugs, this dependence is exactly the "stuff" the analyst craves, his "monkey," as it were (Dehing 1981).

Analysts then are no less patient-addicted than patients are analyst-addicted. If they do not get their regular dose of patient, they risk showing withdrawal symptoms. It is not by chance that the most successful professionals in the field claim that they feel well only toward evening, when their need to nourish has been satisfied.

This reciprocal dependence—which is anything but surprising when we consider that it is implicit in the mother–child relationship upon which the analytic relationship is based—is healthy for the patient, not only because it is the ideal cement for the therapeutic alliance, but also because the discovery that the analyst needs the patient, that he feels necessary in a regressive relationship, brings the patient back to his very earliest experience of relationship. However, introduced into that far-off event is a new and extraordinarily propulsive element. The repetition compulsion, instead of producing yet another identical performance of the old script, this time has to deal with an important variation.

During the very early phases of development, the child is certainly capable of understanding how necessary others are to him, but he is not really able to understand that he is also necessary to others. On the contrary, everything seems to confirm his idea that he is not necessary to anyone. How could it be possible for someone who needs everyone to be necessary to anyone? In his primitive logic there is no place for such concepts as reciprocity, interdependence, or mutual need. To become in turn necessary is a need and a project, liberation and revenge in that infantile view according to which only one who is needed does not need others; only one who nourishes has no need to be nourished.

Adler based his metapsychology upon this concept of reality and its plan conceived and carried out to escape this congenital inferiority. That intolerable condition of inequality, the relationship of the dwarf to the giant, which the child experiences in relation to parents and subsequently to all adults, remains in the adult as an awareness of limitations in relation to others, society, and reality in general, threatening at any instant to cancel the individual. This is the origin of the desperate, vital need to affirm one's essential role in external reality.

Certainly one's awareness of one's own finite nature in an infinite reality can never be suppressed, except in delusions of grandeur, mystical ecstacy, or hallucination. However there is the danger of this existential knowledge being translated into an incapacity to interact with others, with any other, in a real relationship, when the other in oneself is perceived in the relationship as annihilating from the moment it appears on the psychic horizon. This is the myth of Medusa, who turned men to stone if they dared to gaze upon her, rewritten by Sartre (1944) as the fate of every human relationship. The simple appearance of the other can transform the ego from subject to object, degrading it, alienating it from itself.

However, it would be well to remember that, apart from philosophical considerations, our civilization has in effect evolved in such a way as to perpetuate the Medusa myth. As we have already noted concerning creativity, in one way or another the social order demonstrates that it has more need of objects than subjects, more need of automatons than of people. It is difficult to feel necessary when our roles, as both producers and consumers, appear to us to be constantly guided and programmed; thus is the collectivity, which has taken upon itself the task of confirming the ancient, depressing relationship of the dwarf to the giant, confirmed in the neurosis I have called the frustration of insignificance (Carotenuto 1980).

In Bontempelli's *Minnie la candida*, a friend of the main character convinces her that some of the small fish darting about in a tank in a shop window are "electric" — that is, artificial — but so perfect that it is impossible to tell them from real fish. Encouraged by Minnie's ingenuousness, her friend goes even further. There are, he says, also artificial *men* in circulation, so perfect so as to be indistinguishable from real men, and who knows how many of them we have come across on our walk. As a result, Minnie closes herself up in the house and will neither answer the phone nor open the door when her concerned friend comes to see her. She screams from behind the door for him to go away and suddenly it occurs to him that the trouble with Minnie is that she suspects him of being an artificial man, an automaton. The truth, however, is that Minnie believes that she herself is not real, that she is an electric, artificial person. And for this reason she throws herself out of the window (Bontempelli 1928).

In analysis many patients experience a real relationship for the first time in their lives, for previously, following the repetition impulse, they had always entered into relationships in which they were dependent to the point of practically eliminating recompense, thus continuously confirming their primitive, depressing concept of the relationship. This includes the most recent choice, that of going to an analyst, which certainly in the eyes of the new patient presents the connotations of yet one more repetition of placing oneself in the hands of another, infinitely more powerful. However, this latest

39

choice will open his eyes for the first time to reciprocity, not glimpsed or seen in the abstract as in the past, but palpably and tangibly experienced.

It is curious that analysis, famous as an imitation of an emotional relationship, should be destined to represent for the patient the very first authentic relationship. And yet, if authenticity is created by and draws nourishment from reciprocity, then it is right that it should be so. Whether or not the analyst attempts to hide his own feelings, it will not be long before the patient realizes that his partner has invested energy, emotion, and suffering in that relationship, in the same way that the patient has (Tauber 1954). Then the patient will understand why, at the beginning of the therapy, the analyst said, "I know when we begin, but I cannot say when we will finish." There is in the analyst, as there is in the patient, an unconscious desire to continue the rapport endlessly, in spite of all the established rules.

To return to our history, the first to speak of hypnotism rather than magnetization was the English physician James Braid (Belfiore 1928, pp. 48ff.; Servadio 1938, pp. 15–18; Marks 1947, pp. 79–82; Podmore 1963, *passim*; Ehrenwald 1966, pp. 50–56; Ellenberger 1970, *passim*; Hunter and Macalpine 1971, pp. 906–910; Chertok and De Saussure 1973, pp. 49ff; Ehrenwald 1976, pp. 243–250). A surgeon, he tended even more than Mesmer to prefer the concrete, tangible, and circumscribed reality of the human body. Instead of looking for the explanation of the magnetic phenomenon in the cosmos, Braid looked for it in that microcosm which is the human organism. He described the mechanism of inducing sleep as a luminous stimulus, able to capture and hold the patient's attention through the retina, then striking a particular area of the nervous system, causing the entire organism to fall asleep within a quarter of an hour (Hunter and Macalpine 1971).

It would be superfluous to point out how the need to objectify — all the more powerful because added to cultural pressures was the psychotherapist's desire to protect himself from this mysterious and disturbing relationship — won in the end with Braid's hypothesis, after the intuitions of Abbot Faria and Puységur put the poor psychotherapist at risk.

Underlining this objectification in an absolutely emblematic and symbolic way is the instrument adopted by Braid to induce hypnosis: from among all the suggestive techniques available, he chose to use a brilliant object placed about forty centimeters from the patient's nose, from which the patient was obliged not to remove his gaze.

Objectifying the therapeutic relationship meant not only protecting the therapist behind technical methods and apparatus, but also reducing the patient to the status of an object. This was all well and good as it accomplished in a perfectly consistent manner an operation whose more or less conscious aim was the removal of all emotional charge which might have rendered the relationship uncontrollable, or at least worrisome. It is infinitely less difficult to control objects than human beings. How many Gepettoes would rather procreate puppets than children? The most frightening tale ever told is the legend of the Golem, for what could be more terrifying than the idea that a mechanism of our own making could gain autonomy, to the extent of actually revolting against its creator? Although according to Genesis, this is exactly what the first man did.

This fear of being overcome in relationships with others in their capacity as human beings, with the resulting need to deal exclusively with objects, has actually come to be considered a positive value in contemporary Western society. (We *are* what we possess, *are* the step we occupy on the social ladder, *are* our professional status.) We need go just one step further to consider it a fiscal value, as is the case in the United States where annual income is often indicated by the way social introductions are made.

Relationships are often formed between facsimiles, between photographs, between business or identification cards, and are thus facsimile relationships. We have been educated in this way since early childhood. The patient work of indoctrination would never succeed so well if it did not find the ground already prepared, if in early childhood one had not learned at one's own expense to be wary of authentic relationships, in which the currency of exchange is feeling or emotion.

This is the only currency the child has to spend in the earliest phases of its existence. And indeed the child spends it lavishly, squanders it. It is the adult, unfortunately, who will not or cannot, repay the child in kind, as the child expects. A dedication as total as a child's is physiologically impossible for an adult, who at the very least has learned to restrain feelings and emotions. Thus the response to the child's emotions will inevitably be experienced as a cold shower, leading to frustration (Ferenczi 1931, p. 129).

These experiences leave their mark and are much more formative than any of the didactic methods subsequently applied. A dark fear of the emotional relationship, a need to remain safely far away from frustration, will remain inside anyone who has experienced the violence of emotion as defeat.

It should not be surprising that those who have chosen to concern themselves with the human soul — the psychotherapists — also harbor the secret hope of being able to do it, so to speak, from on high, in the manner of nuclear researchers who manipulate radioactive substances exclusively by means of sophisticated mechanical arms which they control in safety from behind a transparent wall capable of absorbing the harmful radioactivity.

Freud himself, who, genius apart, had the courage to look for the first time directly at some of the most disturbing realities (the phantasms of the unconscious, for instance, skeletons in the closets of our past), when confronted with transference felt the need at least initially if not to negate it, then at least to point it out as a characteristic resistance to analytic treatment, a spoke in the wheel, a new system of diversion excogitated by the patient at the moment a repressed conflict was about to be revealed (Freud 1895, pp. 302–303).

Obviously, it is not the fear of being loved which disturbs the sleep of the psychotherapist, but the fear of being induced to respond to that love, of having to respond to emotion with emotion. "Love, that excuses no one loved from loving," and "Love is begotten by the love of another,"[1] warned Dante, and before him, Andrea Cappellano, in the twenty-sixth rule of his treatise, De Amore, "No love shall decline another,"[2] and Frà Giordano da Pisa, "No one feeling himself loved by another will not be led to love that person boundlessly."[3] Even St. Catherine of Siena had something to say about this: "The soul naturally tends to love its lover."

No one dealing professionally with psychological problems should entertain the illusion that one can immunize oneself against emotions and feelings by simply banishing them. Turning once more to

---

[1] Amor che a nullo amato amar perdona.
Amor acceso di virtù sempre altro accese.

[2] Amor nil posset amori denegare.

[3] Non è nullo che, sentendosi amato da alcuno, ch'egli non sia tratto ad amare lui incontanente.

the field of literature, I shall quote an author a bit closer to us in time. Raymond Radiguet, in describing one of his characters, wrote:

> As every organ develops or atrophies according to its activity, by dint of mistrusting his heart, he had very little. He believed that he was strengthening himself, that he would acquire a patina of bronze, and instead he destroyed himself. Deceiving himself totally as to the goal to be reached, he admired in himself more than anything else this slow suicide. He believed that he would live better. But till then he had found only one way to stop his heart, and that was by dying. (Radiguet 1924).

Since it is unfeasible for emotion to atrophy, the only hope left the psychotherapist is that of sterilizing the relationship with the patient by means of that most powerful of antiseptics, its scientific nature.

That hope unfortunately has been frustrated up until now, for this discipline, although it enjoys considerable favor among people of culture, has scant credibility before the supreme courts of scientific objectivity (Farrel 1981).

We have to admit, this is not without reason. Even an epistemology of Galileo's time would hesitate to confer scientific status to theories which make no provision for any degree of repeatability of the experience, because it is a fact that psychoanalysis considers every clinical case unique. Imagine then the reaction of more sophisticated and exigent epistemologies—Popper's, for example—which to the criteria of verifiability is added the so-called falsifiability.

It would be difficult to indicate with any precision what observations could falsify the Freudian theories of repression and the meaning of dreams, or Adler's theory on the inferiority complex. Indeed, Popper has shown that, from an epistemological point of view, neither Freud's nor Adler's psychoanalyses have all their papers in order (Popper 1963, pp. 34ff).

Only before the epistemologist P. K. Feyerabend do we all, Freudians, Jungians, Lacanians, and so on, get off lightly. In fact, Feyerabend's epistemological anarchy denies that an objective scientific method exists, or could exist, and compares science to an ideology or religion whose influence on contemporary humanity is analogous to the influence Christianity once had on society (Feyerabend 1971, pp. 6ff; Feyerabend 1978, pp. 409–426).

43

Five

Psyche and Soma

The extensive experimentation conducted on techniques of hypnosis has provided us with many observations on certain phenomena of great interest to psychology—the relationship between psyche and soma—phenomena which even today have not been satisfactorily explained.

In order to understand why these explanations cannot be considered completely satisfactory, we need merely consider the famous blister phenomenon. A person in a hypnotic trance is informed by the hypnotist that the coin about to be placed on the person's arm has been made red-hot. Of course this is not true; it is not by torture that the hypnotist induces the subject to talk. Yet, when the innocuous coin is removed, the classic blister appears on the arm of the "victim" (Certok 1979).

The only thing clear at this point is that the blister, not directly caused by an external act of aggression cannot be considered a real lesion or wound (as might a third-degree burn), but merely an organic response (insulating the layer of "injured" skin with a cushion of serum). There is nothing miraculous in the fact that suggestion should succeed in triggering a reaction, simulating a real stimulus. A false alarm results initially in the firemen rushing out, although there is actually no fire.

However, this explanation does not thoroughly make clear the nature of the mechanism that makes possible this and other analogous phenomena. As far as we know, organic responses such as the mobilization of antibodies in the presence of fever, the coagulation of blood, or the healing of a wound are automatic. It is pointless in such cases to say that the will of the hypnotist has replaced that of the person hypnotized, because this type of process is not ordered by anyone's will. As for the word "suggestion," it explains absolutely nothing. Whenever has a *thought* substituted for a *physical stimulus*? Into what secret control room do the hypnotist's suggestions penetrate? How is it that he succeeds in enabling the patient to control, in a trance, processes before which he is absolutely powerless in a normal state?

The fact is that the entire problem of the psychosomatic relationship is very far from being resolved. We know that between the two spheres there is a very strong interdependence. However, we have only just begun to decipher this complex mechanism.

Physicians continue to find confirmation of the importance of the patient's attitude toward illness as an element in recovery. As for the attitude toward therapy we need only remember the very familiar placebo effect in order to reveal its determinant role. Even a declared enemy of psychoanalysis, the famous Nobel Prize–winning (1960) immunologist, Medawar, recently announced that he is developing an immunological prophylaxis for tumors which takes into consideration the patient's psychology, explicitly making his own the hypothesis that in almost all illness the nonconditional surrender of the immune system has a psychic origin. In other words, it is not just probable, but has been conclusively proven, that by means of mysterious channels the psyche influences even the more autonomous workings of our organism.

Even yoga, particularly in the form imported and practiced in the West, and kindred techniques present both the possibility of conscious control of organic functions which are normally outside the power of our will (for example, by means of a special training one can actually learn to control one's heartbeat) and the difficulty of explaining theoretically those acquired abilities within the framework of our scientific knowledge.

Up until the advent of psychoanalysis and the discovery of the unconscious, another aspect of hypnotic experiments remained a mystery. This is related not so much to the psychosomatic relationship but to the mnemonic capacities of the patient. While these were extolled because the subject, during "magnetic sleep," was able to remember events from the distant past and from childhood, they were also compromised by the strange fact that once the patient came out of the trance, he remembered nothing of what he was ordered to do by the hypnotist — even if this did not prevent him from following those orders to the letter.

Where then did those messages end up, where were they hidden, since they left no trace in memory, although they dictated subsequent action?

In order to explain this contradictory aspect of post-hypnotic amnesia, it was necessary to arrive at an understanding of just how little of our psychic life is lived, so to speak, in the full light of day, and of how consciousness represents — like the altogether too-frequently cited tip of the iceberg — only a fraction of something larger.

It was necessary then to postulate an unconscious psyche. Only in this way could what today we call subliminal messages be explained, because they pass under the threshold of consciousness. Eluding the control of the ego, these messages (sensations, stimuli, information, even orders and prohibitions) go directly to those remote places where so much of our behavior is determined — above all, that type of behavior which we are the first to be surprised at and of which neither the moment before nor immediately following, could we have imagined ourselves capable. It is for the same reason that in a waking state we are not able to remember these messages. They are, we might say, "warehoused" without having been recorded or catalogued. And so we are not able to withdraw them from our memory's depository.

Much of the phenomena — perhaps all, if we refer only to the authentic — with which parapsychology deals has to do with the mysterious channels which in theory reduce distance more than any other method of communication, but which very few are actually able to utilize. This was one of the reasons why Freud abandoned hypnosis as a possible "royal road" to the unconscious.

It is probable that these faculties, which today, because of their rarity, we call paranormal, were common enough long ago. However, with the evolution of civilization they were used less and less until finally they atrophied (Nietzsche 1888–1889, p. 86). As the means of long-distance communication became more and more available to us, the less we needed to resort, for example, to telepathy. Already at the dawn of culture, language (verbal communication) with its ever more refined codes of interpretation, including the possibility of lying, or at least of keeping hidden our true thoughts (an option that empathic communication does not permit), must have led *Homo sapiens* to deactivate mechanisms for which they had no further use.

We might say that contemporary people use a considerably reduced part of their potential psychic energies. Any psychological training tends to attempt to recover energies not utilized, because psychic energy is the real blood which keeps us alive, the true lymph of the human organism. Of course, in the psychoanalytic context, it is not a question of recovering paranormal powers, which were certainly not the only ones repressed. Instead it is a question of liberating energies blocked in sterile repression of anachronistic, unresolved conflicts.

In 1843, James Braid was converted to magnetism, renamed it hypnotism, and decided to confer upon it scientific and objective status. That is a dream which—fortunately for the patient—has even today not become reality. Our discipline eludes attempts at objectifying, probably because it does not deal with objects.

A similar recurring dream is that of the unifying theory. Although every author promises himself to produce the theory to end all theories, an infinite number of schools continues to exist, fortunately for the psychotherapist.

In fact, it is thanks to just this characteristic—which, by the way, our discipline has in common with the other humanistic sciences, including epistemology which, by right, should make all other sciences toe the line—that the psychotherapist may espouse the metapsychology which most pleases him. It is a love match, for the psychotherapist does not make a judgment based on rational criteria, but instead chooses the one which best suits him, the one that strikes a responsive chord.

Braid, when conferring the status of scientific objectivity on hypnotic therapy, obviously had to remove all the subjective elements contaminating Mesmerian theory. He began by eliminating the term "fluid," in the hope that by suppressing the term, he had suppressed the concept as well.

It was a vain hope; even today, we find the fluid alive and well on the Freudian psychoanalyst's couch and in the Jungian psychologist's armchair, the contemporary term for it being libido or psychic energy. It would be difficult to deny that this energy—or libido—circulates in the psychoanalytic setting. Analysts obtain proof of it every time that intense, harmonious flow is interrupted by some unexpected external event—usually a telephone call—when it is upset and dispersed. However brief the interruption, a certain amount of time and much goodwill is required (on both sides) before the free but ordered flow is reestablished.

Braid, however, had his reasons for denying it. Because its founder knew how to placate the idiosyncracies and fears of his medical colleagues, it was possible for "Braidism" to emerge and assert itself.

Mesmer, too, was a physician. However, it is not by chance that his medical thesis dealt with the relationship between medicine and astrology. Braid preferred to ignore the harmony of the celestial spheres and espoused the magnetism of phrenology. Thus, the relationship studied was between the patient's psyche and the patient's organism; magnetic sleep was self-induced, and the therapist was not directly involved.

But we should not wax too ironic regarding this persistent and exclusive focusing on the relationships between brain and organism, nor should we minimize the positive effects it produced, both directly and indirectly. Whatever the secret reasons were for Braid's opposition to the repugnant fluid, the result was a focusing on the internal dynamics of the individual's psychic energy. He did not care to see the flow between therapist and patient. As compensation, however, he glimpsed with promising clarity the equally reciprocal relationship between psyche and soma (Hunter and Macalpine 1971).

Even today, phenomena such as depression and the various moods in the same individual at different times of the day are rightly taken as proof of the capacity of psychic energy to influence us physically. A surprising confirmation of this assumption—if one is necessary—was obtained during the Second World War in the Nazi concentration camps. Those who survived the inhuman conditions were above all those who had been imprisoned for political reasons. The fact that their psychic energy was generated and sustained by an ideal positively influenced their capacity to resist deprivation and illness (Bettelheim 1960).

The power of the psyche over the soma is revealed by a phenomenon that occurs in relationships between two individuals. As long as we are familiar only with the physical aspect of another, it seems to us to represent a person sufficiently inspiring like, dislike, or indifference, even allowing us to deduce with reasonable approximation what that person is like inside. However, once we enter into a relationship with the other, as our familiarity grows, not only does psychological aspect become more important, it even succeeds in modifying physical appearance. In love in particular we cease to see a face, a body, as they really are but see them only in the form our psychological attraction gives them.

Regarding the Braidian approach to hypnotism and the psychosomatic relationship, it was thanks to the utilization of those techniques and the development of those intuitions that in the second half of the nineteenth century two French physicians, Briquet (Ellenberger 1970, pp. 142–143) and the great Charcot, were able to classify hysteria among the neurological illnesses, attributing to psychic causes the clearly somatic manifestations of such mysterious ills as migraine, catalepsy, paralysis, and so on. Of course, neither the sterile uterus, as hypothesized by the ancient Greeks and Romans, nor the demon, as was believed in the Middle Ages, had anything to do with hysteria nor did wounds or organic disorders; emotions, passions, conflicts, and frustration were the causes.

It goes without saying, even today, that in such cases, when the ritual examinations and analyses have not produced any significant results, one turns to the psychotherapist, logically supposing that it is a question of a somatic conversion of some psychological conflict. Of course, it is possible—at least in theory—that one day an organic pathogenetic agent or drug will be discovered even for hysterical or obsessive neuroses. This would imply that the psychotherapists would sincerely admit that they had extended the effect to include the cause of the illness, confusing cause with effect and thus falling victim to a misunderstanding which is anything but new to the history of medicine.

However, at present such a discovery has not been made, and we can say that not only is psychotherapeutic treatment the only one which appears to produce positive results, but that also, theoretically, the psychological approach is to date the only one which has provided a reasonably acceptable explanation of these phenomena.

In the end, credit goes to Braid for having accredited to the psyche of the patient, and thus to every human being, extraordinary, unsuspected, and usually unused abilities to control the organism, abilities which are completely independent of the presumed thaumaturgical qualities of the physician, even though the patient/therapist relationship was shortchanged in the process.

Mesmer's fluid, however objectified, homogenized, and depersonalized, was nevertheless a bridge between the magnetizer and the magnetized. Once that bridge had been blown up, nothing more passed between them, and the patient was left alone with his drama and his anxiety.

The patient would not remain so for long, for in spite of Braid's anathemas, the therapist also feels a secret need to play a more essential and prestigious role in that drama, as well as a mysterious attraction toward the dangers implicit in an involvement of this sort.

Six

Empathic Suggestion

August Ambroise Liébeault, a French physician who, like Braid, was not content simply to practice hypnotic therapy but wanted to give his interpretation of it (Liébeault 1889), was one of the first to give the therapist back the role of partner to the patient and no longer instrument, at the same time restoring the importance of the therapist's personality which Braid had denied.

On the technical level, Liébeault required that the patient fix his attention no longer on just any luminous object, but on the eyes of the hypnotist. Consequently, theoretically, he did not refer to "self-induced sleep," but to "sleep induced by suggestion." Thus, the patient/therapist relationship was reestablished, a relationship that actually lasted well beyond the moment the patient awakened from the hypnotic trance.

It was naturally a strongly unbalanced relationship, even to the point of being a form of subjection, since the patient did nothing but submit to orders. Liébeault's suggestive technique was imperative, both when he ordered the patient to sleep and when subsequently he ordered him to be cured of his illness.

It has been said that the type of client Liébeault dealt with determined his choice of technique and theory. They were humble individuals, soldiers, farmers, simple workers, used to taking orders. However, it is important to remember that the type of client he had was not the result of circumstances beyond his control, but the foreseeable result of a precise strategy. In fact, when he had earned enough money to be independent, Liébeault began proposing two alternatives to his patients—traditional treatment upon payment or hypnotic treatment free of charge. It is not difficult to guess which they chose. It is even less difficult to imagine the social level of a clientele recruited with such a incentive. The well-to-do, true to a caste eccentricity, usually judge the worth of professional performance by the fee they are asked to pay. We might also add that only the simple souls of that time (around 1860) were not ashamed of preferring a physician reminiscent of the healer of bygone days, part exorcist and part magician.

Thus, Liébeault was considered something just short of a saint by his patients and little more than a charlatan by his colleagues. Justice was eventually awarded him by the followers of the so-called School of Nancy when they proclaimed him their spiritual father.

Possibly the main reason for his ostracism was the mistrust inspired by the term "suggestion," upon which Liébeault based his theory. Suggestion describes both true deception inducing a false perception as well as certain *real* manifestations induced by emotional, nonrational factors. Thus, anything resulting from suggestion of any sort is discredited as misleading, deceptive, and unfounded (Poll 1967).

In all truth, it does not take a great deal of acumen to distinguish one from the other. Consider a case in which both were present: the famous professional accident associated with the great illusionist, Bartolomeo Bosco. According to the story, a woman in the audience died—apparently by drowning—during a performance in which the prestidigitator created the illusion that the orchestra section was flooded. Whether the episode actually occurred is not clear; however, what is clear is that if it did, we are obliged to consider fictitious and illusory the flooding of the orchestra, but dramatically real the death of the spectator.

It is often the case that the "imaginary" seems to counteract the "real," as if the two were mutually exclusive, as if when one appears there is no longer room for the other. Even Freud, who based all his research on psychic reality, when he realized that some of his patients' childhood memories—the famous traumatic seductions, which he considered the origin of obsessive neuroses such as hysteria—were not episodes that had really occurred, feared that they would automatically lose all etiological value (Freud 1985, pp. 264–265).

However, the confusion was short-lived, and it was not long before Freud's intuitive capacity allowed him to regain the upper hand: those fantasies expressed the patients' unconscious desires, and as such had an absolutely concrete importance in their lives.

Suggestion has always been, and will continue to be, a fundamental factor in communication. Today, as in the past, it is impossible to attribute the success of some of the great demagogues and leaders of the populace exclusively to the soundness and persuasiveness of their arguments.

The fact is that man is more sensitive to the form of communication than to its content. I am not alluding here to the bag of verbal tricks that since the time of Homer, has been the heart and soul of the lively discipline of rhetoric, considered an art, having as it does a Muse, Polyhymnia (although it is Muse in common with lyrical hymns). However, it is not rhetoric that is relevant here, but rather something that has nothing to do with the verbal aspect of communication, flowing below the discourse and instantaneously striking its mark with infinitely more skill than the most practiced orator.

This phenomenon does not amaze the psychoanalyst, who knows only too well that emotions and not reason are transmitted on that wavelength. And if it is true, as we have said, that culture tends to cause one's capacity for empathic communication to atrophy, it is equally true that a culture based on affection does the exact opposite, functioning as it does at a point in our individual evolution before the appearance of language.

We are once more referring to that very early phase in emotional life of interpersonal relationship, the symbiotic bond of the child to its mother. In order to describe the formative value of this very early experience, we might borrow the ethological term "imprinting." Ethology is a discipline we would do well to consult every now and then for indirect but reliable testimony, particularly regarding cases where it is unclear whether a specific mechanism should be attributed to instinct or to learning. It is imprinting which is responsible for that communication's appearing forcefully, not only in life's crucial moments, but as a behind-the-scenes constant in all our relationships.

Communication is in itself ambiguous because, as Watzlawich revealed in *Pragmatics in Human Communication* (1967), aspects of both content and context exist in all messages. It is the latter of the two which defines, with the contribution of analogical language, the content, revealing thus the real intent of the sender. This is the point at which the ambiguity of communication begins: what is asserted verbally can be negated on another level.

In the analytic relationship, even though there is usually a lot of talk and verbalization, the most effective communication by far is actually empathic because at that level the primary child/mother relationship is once again evoked. It is not so much the words that count as their emotional aura, just as it is not as important to talk about the past as it is to allow its emotional content to be revealed through the patient's present attitude. The analyst is, or should be, able to deduce the patient's background from behavior, in a process Freud called "constructions in analysis" (Freud 1937–1939), a process analogous to the historical reconstructions done in archaeology by means of the interpretation of fragments.

If, for example, a patient in earliest infancy (a period not remembered) was frustrated by a depressed mother who was incapable of sending emotional messages, thus experiencing early on emotional life as a source of suffering, his approach to all emotional situations will resemble a hand reaching toward something red-hot, hesitant, ready to withdraw. He will never admit emotional involvement and will defend himself from it because his personality has been structured on the equation, feeling = suffering. Or he may perceive the object of his affection as something persecutory because his most crucial experience was lived in pain.

However, the diametrically opposed attitude is also seen by the analyst as having the same origin. Patients who are insatiable on the emotional level are those who have received nothing from the mother and are infinitely avid for compensation.

These early emotional experiences are also the basis of the so-called state of falling in love. In this case, however, the experience is more evolved than the original relationship with the mother, as it is in the oedipal phase that a third party, a figure indispensable for the development of authentic affection, enters. In love, the third party is not an intruder; his presence is not an inauspicious event which complicates things. Rather, it is essential, the condition *sine qua non*, and if it did not exist it would have to be invented, evoking at least its ghost, because the model on which falling in love is based is in fact the oedipal triangle (Hillman 1972).

Radiguet's novel, *The Ball of Count Orgel*, which we have already cited, centers entirely on the intuition of a tripartite love structure, which has nothing whatever to do with the traditional *ménage à trois*.

The husband is able to love his wife only when the other man appears, and for this he is grateful, almost loving the other for forcing him to love.

However, analysis, as we have already revealed, is not limited simply to probing the oedipal triangle, but goes even deeper, down to the foundations of the patient's emotional history, to the symbiotic relationship with the mother. If in that relationship there has been a breakdown, usually due to a depressed mother, we will have a very difficult patient, because that psychological wound goes back even further than the Oedipus complex. In the oedipal phase the child discovers and suffers from jealousy. But although this experience is undoubtedly a frustrating one, he is able to glimpse a way out: the third party (the father) already represents "others," the external world. This presence, which causes so much suffering, also provides an opening to a new vision, more complex and thus richer, causing the child to perceive the possibility of directing libidinal energies in another direction, satisfying them with other love objects.

In the primary relationship, however, this child is *bound* to the mother, in spite of the frustration this causes. Only in this way can certain sadomasochistic versions of the couple relationship, the origins of which are in the primary relationship, be explained. Thus, these early experiences are fundamental ones, and for this reason we must recognize that ours is essentially an emotional and not a cognitive language. Love, like panic, can be transmitted without words (Balint 1968).

It is an unfortunate fact that the emotional domain enjoys very little credibility in our culture, whose history has been a long and never-resolved conflict between opposing needs. Observe the difficulty in our culture of a confident approach to emotions and the recurring temptation to banish emotions as threatening to the established order. There are those who speak of "removal." The correct term is "repression," which in any case has anything but succeeded. Those wielding power are very much aware of this; in fact, it is precisely upon the emotions that they play in order to obtain consensus or discourage dissent.

The fact is that the road to repressing emotion, most frequented by those whose task it is to "educate" (beginning with the family, but including the institutions which subsequently back it up and substitute for it), especially in the Occident—which must necessarily include traditional Japan—cannot fail to derive from deep-rooted collective cultural choices.

The most obvious result of this repression, which for obvious reasons begins *after* earliest infancy, is that our emotions fatally conserve infantile connotations, those belonging to the only period in which they were allowed to be shown. It is for this reason that each time we give in to our emotions we have the impression of somehow regressing to infancy. Our emotions have not become adult, they have not grown apace with the rest of us. They have been stunted in the same way that the bound feet of Chinese women once were.

We might observe here that this repression is more evident in men than in women because it begins for the male at an earlier age. It is the male child who must free himself earlier from the primary relationship with the mother in order to differentiate himself from her and objectify this difference. The female child's motivation to objectify is not so urgent or radical, since in her case it is possible to continue identifying with the mother without danger of jeopardizing sexual identity. The fact that man's capacity to relate is often inferior to woman's is probably due to the fact that the male child is forced to distance himself too soon from the mother.

Separation is one of the fundamental experiences the child is forced to go through in the uroboric relationship with the mother. It is a painful experience which unfortunately will be repeated *ad infinitum* in the course of the individual's life, for the personal history of every one of us is a series of meetings and separations.

Birth, after all, is already a separation. The individual develops inside a womb which encloses and protects. The moment of birth comes as a trauma of separation, a tearing away, an expulsion. There now exist delivery techniques which attempt to render separation from the mother more gradual, avoiding the violence of suddenly plunging the infant into an environment so different from the mother's womb by reproducing on the outside the same conditions of darkness, silence, and physical contact the infant had experiences inside the mother. However, even today in our clinics the infant is soon taken away from the mother and kept away for long periods during the day, physical contact being provided only during feeding times. To this exception to the rule, no one has dared to object, because the conviction that the mother must nourish the child has been so firmly ingrained in our mentality that it generates — or better still, degenerates into — the widespread prejudice that it is the female who must provide nourishment, even if only with a bottle. What is more important is that the infant can count on a warm and constant presence. But the prejudice has tended to perpetuate beyond specific biological mechanisms a division of roles which in many cases is purely conventional (Dinnerstein 1976).

No cultural device will ever eliminate for the young creature so painful, if necessary, an experience for its growth as the separation from the uroboric matrix. This separation leaves us with a perpetual longing for that happy condition, that Eden from which we were sent out, and together with this nostalgia, the hope (unuttered, often obstinately denied) of one day regaining that lost paradise.

It is this hope that makes every new encounter seem so mysteriously promising. In this light, we might say that the analytic experience presents itself as the Supreme Encounter. It does in fact propose again, with fewer limitations than any other adult relationship, that uroboric condition of perfect communion, nourishment and warmth, protection and the continuous flow of impalpable messages. If it is true, as we have said, that in the analytic relationship silences are as important as words, it is precisely because the model recalled is that of the uroboric Eden, before the fatal original sin of verbal communication. In the analytic relationship, if there is one privileged instrument of communication, it is the eyes, their expression. This is one of the very first methods of communication used by the child to enter into relationship with the world. If the first absolutely cognitive instrument is the mouth, for literally "tasting" reality, there is no doubt that the eyes soon enough become the most sophisticated instrument of learning.

Plato maintained that true education is provided with a look. It is difficult to lie with the eyes. It is next to impossible to wear an expression which communicates something other than what we really feel, because, as it is commonly said, the eyes are revealing. Unfortunately, what is usually meant by education is the simple verbal transmission of a series of concepts, information, and rules, usually modeled on an educational ideal. The result of this, given that verbal communication is ambiguous and often misleading and that eyes cannot lie, is that the lesson will in reality be a twofold message and that one of the two forms of communication can contradict the other.

We now know which of the two is more effective, because often it is action which also contradicts words. It is only too obvious that if a father exhorts his child to loyalty and then behaves himself in a disloyal fashion, there can be little hope for the effectiveness of the exhortation. However, there is a more subtle observation to be made which is both more comprehensive and more specific. When we say that what counts in education is *what we really are and not what we say*, we must remember that "what we really are" is not so much a question of facts opposed to words as a certain image of which we ourselves might not be aware, simply because we have never accepted it, and which the child perceives dimly but irremediably. Fact and behavior can also lie, words and actions can also be consistent and sometimes it is possible to be true to a character we have constructed, but which is, at base, inauthentic, a total lie. Beyond the words and the facts, there is all the rest within us which is not translated into either words or actions and which nevertheless passes, arrives, and is filtered, unnoticed, much more quickly than the actual fact which produces in the child's mind the enormous flaw in the parental image.

Even in the most formal learning situation, there is still an uncontrollable and immediate — in the literal sense — transfer of psychological content, unmediated by the means and canons that might otherwise sweeten and camouflage its sense.

This is true of the relationship between parents and children at the stage when one can begin speaking of education; it is even stronger in the uroboric phase during which this direct transfer of content is not a second level of communication, but the only level. At this point the mother's psychological condition cannot fail in some way to affect not only the present but also the future of the child.

I repeat, "in some way," because it does not seem to me useful to take a rigorously deterministic view. Beyond doubt, as our physical development is conditioned by overcoming certain childhood diseases, so our psychological growth depends on overcoming certain crucial passages in early relationships with the more significant figures of our emotional life. In fact, to treat some cases of infantile neurosis, the *mother* is put into psychotherapy. But it is clear at least in the light of the present state of knowledge, that our discipline does not provide us with incontrovertible models and rules. One might say that the diversity of experience tends to render such theoretical models ever more improbable, supporting instead those who postulate the absolute specificity of each subject, in this case each individual child, and thus the absolute distinctiveness of the outcome of every mother/child situation.

It would, of course, be more convenient if we were provided with ironclad logarithmic tables with which to solve the problems presented by our patients. But then all personal involvement would become superfluous, a very reassuring prospect for some therapists, but for others one that would strip this work of all appeal, rendering it no longer responsive to their personal need—complementary to that of the patient—to reexperience those problems.

However, auspicious or not for the psychotherapist, scientific parameters for the analyst/patient relationship are not available for the very good reason that we do not have them for the model on which it is based: the primary mother/child relationship. It is always to this model that we must refer when continuing the discourse on what occurs between analyst and patient (Balint 1968).

Up until now we have discussed the influence of the mother's psychological condition on the child, but we should not overlook the opposite phenomenon. If the mother, whether she wants to or not, conditions her child in some way, we also know very well how the child, from the time of its birth, conditions the mother. Analogously, we can suppose that the influence between patient and analyst is also reciprocal.

Even if the awareness—that is, knowing the rules of the game—that we must presume every psychoanalyst has (and which we cannot presume every mother has) puts the analyst in a privileged position, it does not prevent the patient's specific human essence from affecting him.

This is perhaps why the history of therapeutic relationships, from Mesmer to the present, reveals so many frustrated and repeated attempts at objectification. It is in the end a matter of legitimate self-defense. The psychotherapist experiences the patient's capacity to affect him as a vague threat to his own psychic equilibrium. He views with envy the physician who, not having to deal with the psyche, can afford the luxury of displaying charisma, prestige, and charm without compromising himself, who can enjoy being stimulated, even gratified, by the devotion and love of his patients without having those sentiments necessarily result in reciprocal analogous attitudes.

However, going further into this problem here would mean going into the subject of countertransference even before we have finished our observations on transference. Our summary of the history of the psychotherapeutic relationship has not gone beyond the threshold of the first of these two complementary phenomena—transference, tenaciously refused as long as possible, then accepted *obtorto collo* as a necessary evil, and finally accepted and actually utilized as an indispensable therapeutic instrument (Orr 1954). We can affirm at this point that the psychotherapist, to be the most effective, not only must not fear the patient, but must also not fear rendering him, even more frightening since one of the therapeutic goals is precisely the stimulation and increasing of the patient's psychological capacities. In the context of fear, this implies increasing the patient's dangerousness.

It is our task to help the patient liberate himself from the fetters which were necessary to "tame the colt" but which now restrain him from expressing himself in full force. We must help him liberate himself from external conditioning, in order that he may become the true author of his own existence, rather than a character in a play written by others.

And the patient's liberation must necessarily be affirmed by the liberty of the therapist. An analyst who limits himself to using predetermined techniques in a dogmatic and impersonal way, and who does not dare to risk personally, either on the creative or the emotional level, cannot give what he himself does not possess. He cannot help anyone attain liberty, because he himself is not free. He is no better than the false educator mentioned above.

Seven

The Therapy of Desire

One of the great figures in the history of dynamic psychiatry is Jean Martin Charcot, member of the Academy of Medicine and the Academy of Science and trusted physician to all the crowned heads of Europe (and at the end of the nineteenth century there were quite a few of them including the Czar of All the Russias) (Ellenberger 1970, pp. 89–102). When Charcot became interested in hypnotic phenomena, his fame was such that official medicine felt compelled to give it some serious consideration. There are experts who owe their fame to a particular area of research, but there are also areas of research which owe their legitimate status to the solid reputations of their researchers. For similar reasons, incidentally, the pioneers of psychoanalysis tended not to proselytize indiscriminately, but sought the adherence of established persons to their cause. Similarly Freud welcomed Jung with open arms when Jung—a university professor, well established in the Swiss upper middle class, and above all not Jewish—supported his theories (Freud feared that anti–semitism could conceivably damage his newfound science).

From 1873 to 1884, Charcot gave lessons in the Salpêtrière, a Paris hospital that had been deserted by his colleagues because it had, after having served as a sort of refuge for wayward girls, become a home for the aged, sheltering thousands of old women, all of whom were considered "mad."

His lessons, which at the beginning concentrated on the illnesses of old age and chronic illness in general, became progressively more concerned with disorders of the nervous system, which evidently interested him more and more as he went on with his observations of the hospital's patients.

It goes without saying that taking an interest in a problem does not automatically imply having found its solution. It does, however, create the most favorable psychological conditions for success.

Having become aware of Liébeault's experiments at Nancy, Charcot also experimented successfully with hypnosis as therapy. What impressed him most was the possibility of artificially creating a functional paralysis, that is, if hypnosis could eliminate a particular symptom, it should also be able to induce it. Charcot was a man with a strong personality, an indispensable characteristic in the practice of hypnosis since the failure of a patient to fall under the charm of the hypnotist means that he will not enter into a trance. The serene awareness of his gift prevented Charcot from perceiving that his experiments were becoming progressively less significant: the patients his assistants brought to the amphitheatre where he held his lessons had been coached to do exactly what was expected of them. They "played his game," giving Charcot exactly what he wanted independent of his deliberate suggestions.

In analytic therapy as well, there is the danger that certain results are due to a similar mechanism: the patient unknowingly satisfies the desires of the analyst. Near the end of his life, Freud maintained that in the analytic relationship the patient is so grateful for the affection and attention received that he does everything in his power to overcome his illness in order to please the analyst. Freud also concluded that analysis is, all things considered, a love therapy in the broadest sense (Rieff 1959).

Personally, I would not in the least be surprised should one day it be proven that the "love that moveth the sun and stars" also moves—in the smaller universe of analysis—the patient to be cured.

In any case, a bond of love or affection is during the course of the analysis surely the only excipient that renders acceptable to the patient interpretations inevitably threatening to his narcissism, since they necessarily unmask things meant to be kept hidden. Only an inept analyst will not be able to resist giving his interpretation before having ascertained that the patient has been won over.

As might be expected of a good anatomist, pathologist, and neurologist, Charcot tended to postulate an organic basis for all disorders. As he had succeeded in attributing to injuries of the brain and spinal cord the origins of symptoms of "alcoholic paralysis" and "tabor-paralysis," so he believed it was possible to attribute to some organ the origins of hysteria. And he identified it as being in the genital area.

We should point out that when we drag in the professional training of a therapist in order to explain his need to deal with organs rather than organisms, we are still only at the threshold of the problem. It would be interesting to see what was present before that necessitated this training. I myself am convinced that a preference for dealing with organs, like the impulse discussed above to objectify the relationship, is motivated by that same dark fear of having to deal with the "other," of compromising oneself in an involvement that could threaten the inner equilibrium achieved with such difficulty. What could more effectively objectify a relationship with the patient than reducing him to a single organ?

The difficulty is that the therapist can, in making this choice, count on the complicity of the patient, who for his own part has a desperate need, albeit unknown to him, to escape responsibility. For the patient attributing to an organ responsibility for a malaise or disorder is the condition *sine qua non* for paranoic mechanisms such as considering oneself assailed from the outside. Only when the "enemy" is located in a precise part, identified and circumscribed, is it possible to project it outside. Only then can one who is unwell identify with all of oneself, *except that one small part*. Apropos of this, a patient of mine, a writer, related in a short fable how the Christian God in his "infinite goodness" had created man who was what he was:

> One day, God, who was All, realized that included in that "All," which was really *all*, was also evil. The fact did not please Him, and in a fit of paranoia, He decided to acknowledge no longer that aspect of Himself which He did not like. He even gave that aspect a name: Adam. And from that day on, He lived happy and contented. But not us, because it is not very pleasant to be the projection of a paranoic god.

The devil then is nothing more than the personification and removal to the outside of an interior persecutor; not just the devil of medieval Christianity, driven from the body by means of exorcism or torture, but the secular version as well, which even Freud found it convenient to utilize from the beginning of his studies, gradually altering it to personify the counterwill of the hysterical, the repressed unconscious, the seducer-father, the repetition compulsion, death. Jung, also, when writing to Freud about his delicate problem, openly invoked the workings of the devil (McGuire 1974).

Expressions like "possessed," "driven," "beside oneself with rage, envy, or lust," are not merely rhetorical; they reveal our unconscious desire, infantile though it may be, to give credence in our own eyes to a more acceptable version of an unacceptable impulse or sentiment, the invader, the stranger, come to take up residence in our home.

Returning to symptoms, illness, and organs, somatization disorders can also be seen as shrewd and uncanny unconscious strategies for localizing and circumscribing the enemy. The most paradoxical example of depicting illness as an external enemy is hypochondria. The life of a hypochondriac is a constant struggle with his own body, with the body experienced entirely as the enemy. The displacement of the persecutor from the interior to the exterior causes total alienation from oneself, as if a person could seriously amputate his whole body.

Displacing the inner persecutor to the outside might also be considered a sort of "return to sender," since the origins of these fantasies were in fact external, born of the introjection of fundamental figures in the reality of the early phases of infant development. Melanie Klein, who has studied this theme in more depth, explains that the infant, when confronted with the disturbing experience of a mother who gives and does not give milk, and unable to comprehend and accept that too complex and contradictory reality, interprets it with two separate figures—one gratifying and the other frustrating.

These two internal figures—the good and the bad—exist in the unconscious and will forever condition the fantasy life. They will be powerfully evoked every time situations implying gratification and frustration occur. We know that the same thing occurs with other figures subsequently introjected (the father-judge, the rival-brother, and so on), but it is probable that the "bad" figure, precisely because it originated in the earliest disturbing experience of "illness," is the most difficult to neutralize. We might say that it is not reducible in the medical sense, but only controllable: we can only focus on it, learn to understand its language, and consider its truth. The first reaction, immediate and automatic, to a frustrating event, is inevitably the reappearance of that old persecutor. Reality hates us, does not love us,. has maliciously set us up for this blow. Only subsequent reflection can bring this paranoic point of view up for discussion and correct it.

When reflection does not take place, preventing correction and if the guilty party cannot be identified as other, or as all the others, we look for it in our own body, isolating it and excluding it from ourselves, in other words, repudiating it, so that it becomes the enemy. Clinical experience offers an example of this need to avoid responsibility every time a patient once again proposes an organic explanation for his discomfort.

There are cases in which no clinical evidence succeeds in having any effect on these convictions, in which we are dealing with a patient for whom it is better not to be harsh because the therapist's persistence could prove more harmful than the patient's. There are those whose existential equilibrium holds up only because of the illness that justifies to them and to others their own inability to accept the possibility of being free and creative. A confrontation with this inability could be so painful and devastating that living a pseudo-existence with illness is preferable to facing the actual problem.

The skill of the analyst consists also in understanding when it is advisable to avoid touching on the patient's neurosis. Phobias, for instance, sometimes represent protection against a more serious ill. The impossibility of leaving the house alone can save a person from the unconscious desire to have an accident. We might add that anyone capable of mobilizing so grandiose a symptom as agoraphobia in order to keep some temptation at bay, can also be capable of mobilizing an equally grandiose punishment for violating the drastic prohibition. To the perverse logic of phobias, there are precise analogies in the religious sphere: the unconscious apotropaisms excogitated by all cultures for avoiding the violation of taboos. Here as well the sacredness of the taboo is extended automatically to the preventive practices, and failing to follow the apotropaic ritual is already a violation of the taboo. In the phobic, an analogous equation is established between the distant guilt for which the unconscious apotropaic strategy has been mobilized (in the case of the agoraphobe, the guardianescort) and the preventive measures adopted; thus abandoning that strategy is one and the same with being stained with the guilt for which it was excogitated. The original sin was never committed, but its dramatic charge, the anxiety now attached to it, its terribleness, has been transferred whole to the preventive prohibition devised to avoid running risks. Failing to respect the prohibition is already a sin and merits the same terrible punishment. Those who feel deserving of punishment will inevitably do their best have it inflicted upon them.

For this reason, good therapy must tend to increase, simultaneously with the patient's awareness, also the strength of his ego, so that at the proper moment he will be able to face the fantasies he fears.

Eight

Defensive Strategies

It was thanks to Charcot's personal prestige that official medicine was obliged to consider hypnosis seriously. However, Charcot, because of his particular concept of medicine, did not perceive the revolutionary significance of some of its aspects, those closely related to transference. That task would fall to someone who for a time was near Charcot at the Salpêtrière, the then-young Sigmund Freud, who had requested and obtained a study grant to follow the progress of the French school of neurology.

Although Charcot had dealt with forces and processes the nature of which seemed considerably outside the sphere of anatomy and physiology, he maintained to the end that lethargy, catalepsy, and somnambulism were caused by modifications of the nervous system when exposed to certain stimuli. All of which, once again, meant looking away from the experiential specificity of the physician/patient relationship in hypnotic therapy.

We might say that from Mesmer to Charcot, the therapeutic relationship — despite the number of psychological elements brought to light by the introduction of hypnosis — had undergone an increasingly rigorous process of depersonalization. We have already mentioned the more or less unconscious resistances which dissuade the physician from assuming an important personal role in the relationship with the patient. The most relevant of those resistances play upon the unconscious desire to avoid being emotionally involved and having to pay the emotional price of any deep, interpersonal relationship. We have seen the distant precedent for this in the uroboric experience where such a negative image of emotivity was formed. We should add here that those motivations for legitimate self-defense leading many to avoid situations which echo back to those remote and painful events can lead others to react in the opposite way. Other physicians (Freud, for example) stoically relive that unresolved drama, obstinately delving into that past of suffering and frustration, in order to bring to light its traces and give meaning to them. This is, incidentally, one of the arguments which can be brought against a determinist view of psychic mechanisms. It is conceivable that what gives meaning to our lives is not what has happened to us by chance, when anything might have wounded us fatally, but instead, the manner in which we have chosen to defend ourselves from those blows.

Constructing for ourselves a suit of armor or the mask of strongman is one possible strategy; if perhaps the most rudimentary, it is also the one most within reach in our society. The strongman is a character, as old as narrative and theater, to which the cinema has given the final touch, electing it absolute protagonist — the one with whom the spectator identifies — transferring it, according to the schematic division of good and bad inherited from popular theater and serial novels, from the "bad guys" to the "good guys." From John Wayne to Marlon Brando, from Clint Eastwood to Alain Delon, the tough guy is a positive hero. Ruthless outlaw or implacable enforcer of the law, cowboy or sheriff, spy or executioner, even before they put on a uniform or espouse a cause, they put on a mask so thick it allows no emotion whatsoever to show, indicating to the spectator that the Real Man is immune to any such unvirile agitations.

However, if we examine the plots of these films, we discover that they invariably are versions of the parable of the man who never gives in to his emotions until one fine day when he runs up against something, or someone, opening a breach in his armor, provoking in him a liberating reaction. At this point, we might be tempted to wish the same catharsis on those of our colleagues whose need to protect themselves from emotions, feared as destabilizing, plays a peculiar trick on them: the defense paradoxically is more destabilizing than the enemy without. That fear, being not at all rational but emotional, dulls their intellectual capacity, compromising their ability to reason.

Consider a recent example. I was discussing with several physicians the disbelieving attitude of many toward the psychologist in the practice of psychotherapy, an attitude which I consider more absurd than persecutory, as it is based on a syllogism which does not hold up, briefly expressed thus: the medical profession is characterized by its therapeutic intention, so, as the intention of psychotherapy is therapeutic, the psychotherapist must therefore be a physician. Not only is this a case of flawed logic akin to assimilating a cow to a chair because both are four-legged, but the opening proposition is in itself erroneous. No activity can be regulated on the basis of its *ends*, but only on the basis of its *means*. A driver's license is not required to travel from Lodi to Milan, but only to travel at the wheel of an automobile. An engineering degree is required for one involved in the construction of a bridge, but not for one who proposes to swim across the river. Within our particular field, if that syllogism were carried to its extreme, all those who attempted to alleviate the depression of another (the good Samaritans of the telephone, spiritual leaders, even parents) could be legally prosecuted for "practicing medicine" without a license. The reaction of the physicians to this elementary argument was a sort of rejection, a rash disavowal of their faith in logic, which had become suddenly a conjurer's trick concealing something.

It seems inexplicable that such simple reasoning should be so difficult to accept by even the most qualified and intelligent of physicians. However, the fact is that the psychiatrist instinctively feels that to accept such reasoning would be an admission that psychotherapy is not a branch of medicine, and consequently an acceptance of the specificity of the psychotherapeutic relationship. It is precisely this specificity which is repugnant to the physician, who would much prefer extending to the psychotherapeutic relationship the same reassuring "objectivity" that allows the surgeon and the internist their neutral, antiseptic attitude.

Freud encountered the same difficulty when he attempted to convince his colleagues that, when dealing with psychotic disturbances, the therapeutic relationship must be based on emotional elements. These same resistances he himself, with considerable courage and effort, had had to overcome. In the *Weltanschauung* of a physician the need to objectify is fundamental, an article of faith and a safety belt.

The hidden motivations leading to the choice of a profession are always the result of an unconscious desire to manipulate external reality. However, when the primary material to be dealt with is humanity—as is the case for the teacher, the lawyer, the magistrate, the politician—then those motivations have also to do with power, the ambition to exercise power over one's fellow man. The physician senses that he can exert that power over his patients, providing that his "scientific" training guarantees his ability to use objective instruments, without fear or unexpected results.

Here then we have another motivation explaining the side chosen by analysts with previous medical training in legislative battles for regulation of the practice of psychotherapy. This is not, as insinuated by some spiteful individuals, a corporate defense in the more negative sense of the term, nor is it a claim to an exclusive "hunting grounds" where the fewer admitted, the better and fatter the pickings. And neither is it a matter of a "patient market" subject to laws of supply and demand. What the medical class feels is at stake is something far more sacred. Attributing therapeutic competency in the area of psychology to those trained in the humanities, placing them on an equal footing with physicians, means devaluing the long scientific training of the physician, in his own eyes as well as in the public's opinion.

Yet Freud, the founder of psychoanalysis, although medically trained, arrived soon enough at the point of confirming that in psychotherapy the elements of cure are not found in the quantity or quality of the therapist's technical, scientific knowledge, but in the emotional dynamics activated in the analyst-patient relationship.

Thus, the disputes over and distinctions between "medical" and "secular" analyses, although seeming to deal with important problems and aspects of the psychotherapeutic process, are in reality fed by the personal problems of the physician faced with mental illness. It is not by chance that up until the time Freud and Jung dedicated themselves entirely to the study and treatment of those illnesses, official medicine confined those suffering from such complaints to psychiatric hospitals, the only case in which the word "hospital" was restored its literal and original meaning as "a place where the ill are sheltered," shedding the modern meaning, "a place where the ill are treated." How could a physician, trained in the cult of the "scientific nature of things," be seriously involved in treating cases which certainly were not in keeping with scientific parameters and unreasonable by definition, since the mentally ill "lost their reason"? Nothing remained but to dismiss them and file them away.

It was probably for similar reasons that classic psychiatry, even after it had been decided to treat mental illness, continued to devise therapeutic methods and instruments reminiscent of the Spanish Inquisition, less in keeping with the Hippocratic Oath than devotion to Our Lady of the Agonies.

It was as though the mentally ill had to be punished for their obstinate refusal to be cured, for their inflexible and proud detachment — once pigeon-holed in a system of classification — from the rules of the game in other branches of medicine, for their continual claim to their own specificity, the absolute uniqueness of their illness. I should point out here that, in this regard, matters have not improved at all since the recognition by medicine of the contribution of psychic factors in curing, actually proven experimentally, for example, by the placebo effect. The confusion between this unconscious desire to heal and a conscious will to heal, the postulation of "bad faith" in anyone "not cooperating with the doctor," causing frustration and resentment in a therapist confronted with a case that would not be resolved, placing his professional ability in question, becomes an indictment of the patient. If psychic factors have importance — and thus, according to a fairly common misunderstanding, a responsibility — in apparently organic illnesses, just think what their weight must be in those illnesses which by definition are psychic!

Of this punitive attitude, electroshock and insulin shock therapies are only the more sensational examples. However, a good deal of pharmacological therapy is an authentic act of aggression against the patient's psychic life; pharmaceuticals are the straitjackets of the psyche. Those who fear the ill person fear him because they do not understand him — we very often fear what appears to us inexplicable — and in order to counter their own fears, they often resort to the use of terror themselves.

Fortunately, among psychiatrists an interpretive attitude has arisen and made headway which involves the therapist in the search for the meaning of mental illness, instead of labeling as senseless the behavior of the patient. The patient emits unintelligible messages because his language is not ours; it is the psychotherapist's task to learn to decode it. This was the extraordinary novelty of the Freudian revolution. The first important clinical case in the history of psychoanalysis — the case of Anna O. studied by Freud and Breuer —

71

is a clear example of how a careful psychological investigation can succeed in making sense out of apparently inexplicable behavior, without however neglecting the search for a historical lack which could be the basis of the illness.

The enthusiasm of the pioneers of psychoanalysis for this revolutionary approach generated an exaggerated confidence in its results. It was even thought that deciphering the message, that is, explaining the symptom, actually coincided with the cure, in the same way that the discovery of the guilty party in a mystery novel meant that the case was solved. We know today that it is not quite that simple. That glowing certitude was a residue of the positivist vision of science in which once the pathogenic agent is discovered, the illness is cured. As in the *Ballo Excelsior*, the Light of Progress in itself is enough to set to flight the specters and demons of Evil — an interpretation of the hermeneutic attitude which falls all too easily under the axes of attentive epistemologists (Grünbaum 1984).

It was at Charcot's school that Freud had his first important intuition: the results of hypnotic therapy were due less to the knowledgeable application of suggestive methods than to a *relationship field* formed between patient and therapist. But Freud's interest in the problem had predated that intuition — we have already seen that it was precisely this interest which led him to attend Charcot's course — and he had already found concrete outlets in an association with another neurologist, Josef Breuer, like Freud Viennese, but fourteen years his senior (Jones 1953, pp. 213–214).

Breuer was the therapist involved in the famous case of Anna O., which is rightly considered a milestone in the history of the psychotherapeutic relationship. In fact, it was in that case that transference and countertransference arose and for the first time stepped to center stage.

We know that Breuer did not succeed in drawing from this case the conclusions which perhaps should already have been evident, leaving it to Freud to light up that abyss in which he saw only mortal danger for therapy (ibid.).

Perhaps Breuer lacked the rare talent for discovery. It is not clear. What is certain, however, is that talent alone is not enough to generate revolutionary discoveries. In fact, Freud — who undoubtedly possessed that talent, and would subsequently demonstrate it amply — regretted having met, during those same years, with a similar "distraction" that led him to comment: "Cocaine has earned me considerable fame, but the better part of it has ended up elsewhere" (ibid., p. 125). He "had missed glory by an inch" (ibid., p. 114). Researching and experimenting on himself the physiological effects of a "little-known alkaloid," cocaine, in the hope of proving its usefulness in the treatment of cardiac disease and nervous breakdown, he concluded that the substance was an excellent anesthetic for gastritis and neuralgic pain, preferable to morphine as it was not habit-forming. He spoke of it with various colleagues and friends, among them the ophthalmologist Carl Koller and then stopped thinking about it. But Koller did not stop thinking about it, and after some experiments on animals, he presented cocaine to the Ophthalmological Congress of Heidelberg as a precious local anesthetic for eye surgery.

The fact is that, in addition to talent, discovery also requires a number of other favorable elements. Too often in the history of science a case is cited in the form of anecdote or a set of happy circumstances, which appeared miraculously in order to provide the researcher with the solution to a problem. But the apple has always fallen from the tree when ripe — even if, until the theory of universal gravity had matured in Newton's head, nothing came of it. It is probable that discovery has also to do with a third factor, that is, a feverish, almost maniacal interest in a given problem, a continuous and exclusive attention, poised ready to give meaning to anything connected to that problem.

The other side of the coin, another aspect of that "state of grace," however, is a singular blindness to anything that appears at first sight extraneous to the problem — somewhat in the same way that while searching for something in particular, our eyes do not focus on, that is, we "do not see," anything that does not resemble the object for which we are looking.

Koller had in mind the problem of finding an anesthetic which would not induce sleep for use in eye surgery (Jones 1953, pp. 121–125). Freud, a neurologist, had other things on his mind, and consequently his name is not connected with the discovery of an ophthalmological anesthesia. However, the connections and significance of the pathological manifestations of a "nervous" nature, as it was called at the time, did not escape him.

73

Breuer as well had a dominating train of thought during the therapy of Anna O. His attention was concentrated on the discovery of the source of the symptom through a historical construction of its manifestations. For nearly three years he tormented himself and his patient with a series of endless interrogations, albeit under hypnosis, in order to wrest for each of the unnumerable symptoms and variations, the places, dates, and circumstances of their occurrence, moving backward in time to their first appearance. He was convinced that the identification of the original trauma would automatically provoke catharsis, that is, cure.

Thus, when it became clear to him that his relationship with the patient had begun uncomfortably to resemble a love relationship, it was not equally clear to him that it was precisely that situation which was the therapeutic factor, the condition *sine qua non*. In fact, like Kant's dove, which considered the resistance of the air an obstacle and imagined it could fly better in a vacuum, Breuer saw transference as an obstacle to continuing the therapy and ended the treatment (Kant 1787, p. 52).

This paradoxical conclusion is not so surprising if we consider that Breuer, besides being aware of his patient's feelings, had also become aware of his own "strange sentiments" for her. He also had to consider that his involvement was placing his marriage in crisis.

It is not difficult today for us to understand how his emotional life might have been influenced by his work. We know that Jung as well experienced this same problem when he had Sabina Spielrein in treatment. In *Diary of a Secret Symmetry* (Carotenuto 1980), I point out that the difficult, alarming, and at times dramatic situation in which the analyst finds himself entangled is due to the very fact that he has chosen an occupation in which emotion is the prime material and tool. We have already seen that an attempt to exorcise this risk can be made by clinging to the hypothetical scientific nature of the profession, but that is an expediency which is less and less feasible. In Breuer's time it was still possible, thanks to the positivistic atmosphere, to theorize as "objective" the approach to so-called nervous disorders. The entire person became an object to be treated in the same way a diseased organ was treated. Nowadays, the physician knows that from the moment he becomes a psychotherapist, he can no longer claim immunity or exemption.

Breuer cut short the therapy because, when he realized that Anna O. was asking too much — that she was asking for everything — he was convinced that he had run into something abnormal and absurd, more unique than rare. He could not have known that this is the rule and not the exception in relationships that recall the primary one. In the earliest relationship with the mother, the child does not and cannot avoid making unreasonable demands, since the need for love is not "reasonable" and has no limits.

Breuer could not have suspected — convinced as he was that the winning strategy of psychotherapy was the restoration to memory of a forgotten trauma — that what inevitably and overwhelmingly reappears in a relationship so charged with emotion is just that sort of love in which the subject is the only subject in the world, a totality of need that pleads and cries and shouts because if not loved, the subject dies.

Forty years later, in a similar situation, Jung did not turn his back either on the patient or the therapy, but decided to see it through to the end, experiencing the alarming difficulties inherent in the psychoanalytic relationship. From that dramatic experience followed the intuitions upon which he subsequently based his theories: the concepts of transference and countertransference, anima and animus, and persona and shadow.

Nine

The Fascination of Emotion

If it is with the case of Anna O., and so with Breuer, that the official history of transference begins, it is to Breuer's friend and colleague, Sigmund Freud, that we owe its theoretical development. Freud saw clearly where Breuer had turned away.

Why did the profound meaning of what had occurred between Breuer and his patient not escape Freud? We have said that this sort of illumination, in addition to an exceptional talent, requires steady concentration on a given problem, a sensitization to everything which in its context might be significant. It would not be out of place then to ask what problems could have interested Freud so intensely.

When we pose questions of this type about a famous person, it is certainly not biographical (or autobiographical) information that is lacking, since it is the theoretical construct which reveals the spiritual itinerary, the unhealed wounds, the individual saga of its author; every metapsychology (like every work of art or philosophy) is a flowing and full response to its creator's personal problems (Carotenuto 1980).

Freud was fascinated by Breuer's situation for the very good reason that he himself also had considerable problems in the area of emotional involvement, in interpersonal relationships. Opting for neurological studies did not at all contradict the need for objectification implicit in his original decision to become a physician. In fact, it confirmed and intensified his choice, for not only does neurophysiology offer to those practicing it the possibility of objectifying the relationship with the patient (at least on a par with other branches of medicine), it is also, in the final analysis, concerned with exactly those problems of interpersonal relationship which are the basis of the medical vocation. And so, working in its favor are both the defense and the attraction. One peers over the edge of the abyss, because the abyss attracts — but from behind the security of the sturdy railing of objectification.

All biographies of Freud describe him as an extremely rigid person, with a tendency to repress all show of emotion, even beyond what was required by his epoch and social class. It is curious that it should be the fate of just such a controlled and austere person to recognize the dimension of emotional involvement in the psychotherapeutic relationship. Curious, but not inconsistent, because the very choice of that armor reveals a vulnerability and thus an extreme sensitivity to emotional experiences. Freud speaks often of his infantile suffering in relation to his parents, without however going into the aspect that interests us most here — that is, the child's response to that suffering in the construction of the persona, even before strictly pedagogical interventions enter into it. However, subsequent development of the important Freudian discoveries sheds some light on those distant events to which we have no testimony, the "prehistory" of the child's development. If we turn again to the theoretical model of the original uroboric dimension and consider that in that early phase of evolution, all good and all evil are experienced by the infant as emotions, we can imagine that a child would conceive of emotions as mortally dangerous, against which it must at all costs learn to defend itself. In the child, the first and most primitive of defensive strategies is that of denying what it fears.

It cannot be by mere chance that Freud maintained that the most painful experience for humans is the loss of the father. It is improbable that, in the depths of his soul, the most disturbing emotion was not the loss of the mother. However, it must have been the prohibition of experiencing the most unbearable of emotions that induced him to cancel out the important and concentrate on the innocuous. The most ancient terror — when the mother was the only, all, reality — invokes the most ancient means of defense: negation.

Thus, we can suppose Freud's own defensive strategy, his rigidity in the face of emotion, originated much, much earlier than the oedipal conflict. It is probable that he experienced so much anxiety in the primary relationship that his entire development was conditioned by it — to the extent that he was induced to create a life-style in which there was no place for emotion. We know that this did not, however, prevent Freud from venturing courageously into that unexplored area he knew to be so treacherous for him. But he never succeeded in changing his style of emotion. Even his literary style was perfectly consistent with his defensive strategy and remained so to the very end, when he had abandoned all hope of ever organizing the entire psychic world with physiological parameters and instruments, as he had attempted to do when he was not quite forty in the work reveal-ingly entitled, "Project for a Scientific Theory of Psychology." If we compare Freud's prose—even in the later works—with Jung's, we cannot help but notice how much the former's is guarded, logically structured, dogmatic, truly the scientific treatise, notwithstanding the daring of certain hypotheses. Between the lines, he makes no allusions, never strikes the reader's fancy, as Jung so often does.

At Charcot's school, Freud gave up forever the comfortable illusion that the psychic life could be traced back to organic phenomena, and, referring to the relationship between Anna O. and Breuer, he did not hesitate to predict what would become the uncomfortable destiny of psychoanalysis: emotional involvement—in other words, transference and its counterpart.

Beginning with the School of Nancy, we have briefly covered the last part of the long history of psychotherapy, pausing at that funda-mental aspect, the relationship between patient and therapist. And we have come to Freud. At this point in our discourse on transfer-ence, as least as regards psychoanalysis, it no longer makes any sense to speak of schools. Not that schools no longer exist—even those not versed in our profession know that pluralism has by now become institutionalized—but because differences in attitudes toward trans-ference lie not between schools, but between individual therapists.

That Freud's discoveries were not destined to form the foundation of just one school was clear from the very beginning of psychoanaly-sis. If Jung could say of himself: "I am fortunate that I am not a Jungian," we certainly cannot call him a disciple of Freud. He became immediately—from the very beginning of their difficult friendship— an interlocutor, on the same footing and with equal weight. Jung, not only the first scientist outside the Vienna circle to be interested in psychoanalysis, was also the first to apply Freudian concepts in treat-ing psychoses. This permitted him, as we shall see, to make new discoveries which enriched and profoundly modified Freudian theory.

Working in a psychiatric hospital, Jung dealt with a very different sort of patient than Freud did, and a different clinical experience cannot fail to result in different perspectives, even at the theoretical level. The relationship with Freud quickly changed from dialogue to dialectic precisely because the exploration of the inner world of the psychotic revealed to Jung aspects and phenomena of the psychic life that were difficult to explain in the context of the Freudian definition and description of the unconscious.

Freud's unconscious, of noble philosophical ancestry (Leibniz, Kant, Schelling, Schopenhauer, Hartmann), was a sort of back room in which a person stored all the psychic contents which have never been, or must never remain, present in consciousness. Above all, these include tendencies and instinctive impulses that were unacceptable or unpleasant and, as such, censored, but attributable in any case in the personal history of the "proprietor," to distant events and experiences, also censored, mutilated, or transformed in the subject's memory.

Freud rightly said that this repressed but not destroyed "material," besides conditioning our conscious life in obscure and impalpable ways, often reappears visibly and legibly in dreams, in lapses, and in parapraxes.

However, Jung, when analyzing the contents of the dreams, fantasies, and ravings of his psychotic patients, with suspiciously increasing frequency found himself face to face with images and structures not easily traced back to the individual experiences of the patient.

Each of us is undoubtedly, at every moment, the product of one's own personal history, especially the period of earliest infancy, which by its precocious nature is so formative. It was inevitable that Freud, pioneer that he was, would opt to blaze a trail into that unexplored territory, leaving to others the task of drawing up detailed maps. Following a parallel road, that is, working with psychotics, Jung had other kinds of encounters, collected other elements, and observed the phenomena from a different perspective. He was concerned not with confuting Freud's discourse, but with integrating it. In order to explain the presence in the individual of oneiric material extraneous to direct personal experience, Jung postulated a collective unconscious, innate, as are certain basic instincts, in which imprinting comes into play, but certainly not produced by imprinting, and inherited by virtue of being inherent in the human species.

When the conquistadors attempted in various ways (not all of them overly Christian) to convert the Aztecs to Christianity, they realized that in the Aztec religion there was already something akin to communion: theophagy. How is it that different races, which had had no previous contact, could have excogitated such similar rituals for entering into rapport with the divine? Why is it that Orpheus was devoured by the Bacchae? Why is it that through the rituals of cannibalism the strength of the hero is appropriated? And why are certain symbols (the cross, for example) found in various cultures that are geographically distant and have never had any contact? Jung's hypothesis was a kind of predisposition to respond analogously to analogous psychic experience, implying a fundamental psychic inheritance shared by all human beings. As the genetic material inherited by every individual does not exclude the genetic material common to the species, so certain structures of our psychic life are not created *ex novo* for each individual, but are a part of the human psyche in general.

This new element which Jung added to the map of the psyche could not fail to influence the concept of therapy. Consistent with that intuition, Jung saw analysis and the interpretation of oneiric (or in any case symbolic) material made together with the patient in a totally different light. It was no longer possible to limit oneself to personal and "private" references, and it was not right to squeeze a patient into his or her own limited history of more or less distant defeats and frustrations. Analysis must include that history because each and every human situation is unique and special. But it must also provide the patient with a broader perspective; every man is also Man, and the events of his life, his problems, his growth, his victories, and his failures can and must be read also in a universal context. It is this perspective that gives meaning to the patient's anxiety, relieving him of the feeling that his fate is absurd, putting him in tune with the great events of humankind, the myths.

Thus, the release from the mother and father figures is extended to the great battle in which each of us must engage to liberate oneself from social conditioning, to assume responsibility for one's own destiny, wherein transgression and original sin signify growth and conquest, the price of which is exile from that restful and happy Eden that precludes any autonomous or responsible choice.

80

From this approach to the interpretation of the patient's dreams, associations, and fantasies, an even more important difference in the approach to therapy as a whole results: that is, instead of limiting itself to the investigation and deciphering of the past, it also and above all looks to the patient's future, by helping him to recover his creativity. Creativity, in the broadest and deepest sense of the word, means the renewal—literally—of one's battle to attain dignity, assume responsibility, and take up the challenge of personally controlling one's own relationship to reality.

Like an "open" symbol, the significance of which does not end in a reference to something precise occurring in the patient's past, therapy allows, even demands, interpretation at various levels. It is the opening of a dialogue between the patient and the deepest and most mysterious part of his being. It does not have the last word and does not provide final answers. And it is right that this should be so, because final answers, answers which placate, are those that collective society offers to us ready-made. They are the answers parents give their children—yes or no, in no uncertain terms; good and evil neatly defined—because that is what the child, who cannot live without certainties, needs. However, growing up, becoming an adult, means giving up certainties and consequently putting to test all the choices made on the basis of those certainties.

This is why a patient in analysis sooner or later experiences crises in relationships. If the patient has embarked on the way leading to authenticity and the partner has remained behind, then that relationship, no matter how adequate it may have been at the beginning, becomes inauthentic. Unfortunately, this involves painful and lacerating choices. But the necessity of being true to one's self is more powerful than any other commitment. And an inauthentic relationship benefits no one, neither the partner, who cannot but be aware of its inauthenticity, nor the children, who intuit the falsity of their parents' union.

Ten

Objectifying Emotion

Despite "top secret" status of certain documents from Freud's archives, it has always been known that the Freudian view originated with two fundamental aspects, the theory of infantile seduction and the theory of seduction fantasies. At first, Freud, believing the accounts of his patients—above all, of his female patients—thought that the origin of neurosis lie in the trauma caused by an attempt at seduction by an adult, usually a parent or brother, when the patient was very young. However, a more careful analysis of those accounts convinced Freud that, in most cases, they existed only in the patient's fantasies. His perplexity, which is understandable enough, was soon resolved by a genuine stroke of genius: it was not necessary to search elsewhere for the causes of neurosis; one needed simply to establish that in the psychic life—and thus the psychic well-being of the patient—a seduction fantasy was as significant as an actual seduction.

In his sensational book, *The Assault on Truth* (1984), Masson, although he was able to consult through professional channels 116 of Freud's letters to Wilhelm Fliess (which up until that time had been off limits to common mortals and ordinary scholars), failed to discover any new insights concerning Freud's theory. However, he did maintain that Freud's entire concept of psychoanalysis was based on an act of cowardice, an authentic Galilean abjuration, *oborto collo* and *pro bono pacis* (Latin being indispensable in ecclesiastic affairs).

The reason for that abjuration? The fear of isolation, if not outright ostracism, in an extremely puritanical social climate. Imagine a father sending his daughter to Freud for treatment if this could seriously be considered the equivalent of admitting that he had seduced her at a tender age.

If, on the other hand, it was a question of the daughter's fantasies, then all remained within the realm of normality. Obviously, if an ill person had fantasies, those fantasies could be nothing more than part of their illness. Again, this echoes Galileo, except for the fact (according to Masson) that Freud, unlike Galileo, would carry to its extreme consequence his small cowardly act by building upon it the theory which has gone down in history as psychoanalysis. It is as if Galileo, still continuing to murmur, "And yet it moveth," had constructed an entire system of astronomy based on an abjuration made under duress.

Why do we say that this sensationalistic book has not contributed anything new, apart from the personal opinions of its author on psychoanalysis? Because Freud's "And yet it moveth," revealed in those forbidden letters, was something considerably less than secret. It has been confirmed that it lasted longer than Masson suspects and was not confided in whispers to a friend, but written down clearly, in black and white. It lasted up to and through his last work, "An Outline of Psychoanalysis," published in 1938.

Freud did not disavow his early intuition on the etiology of neurosis, but integrated and enlarged upon it with a succession of extraordinary intuitions. The fact that, for the patients' families, and consequently for the physician Freud, fantasies of seduction were more acceptable than seduction tout court is not very important — and neither is Masson's preference for a psychoanalysis anchored to concrete and real episodes. The fact that Haydn composed the *Farewell Symphony* in order to please Prince Esterhàzy has nothing at all to do with the quality of the music.

What does count is that the idea of *fantasized seduction*, whatever the theoretical and practical necessity from which it may by chance have been propitiated, changed the face of psychology by introducing the concept of *psychic reality* and paved the way for psychoanalysis by introducing another even more revolutionary and scandalous concept — which is now generally accepted — the concept of *infantile sexuality*. To assert that fantasies of sexual seduction can occur in the child's mind meant declaring that sex was an element of the child's psyche. In a real seduction, the child can only have the role of unknowing victim. In an imaginary seduction, not only is the child

83

the protagonist, he has also written the script, no matter how rudimentary, confused, or distorted his ideas on the subject might be. He desires seduction, provokes it, and is seduced in turn.

All this is essential to our discourse on transference. It is precisely in the analytic work of digging up again the period of infancy, that those emotional and erotic dynamics, the basis of transference, are activated. In the "confessions" of patients in analysis, memories emerge of seductive actions by the child toward the adult, incestuous fantasies which more or less consciously render the child not only consenting to the seduction, but in some way an active collaborator. That the seduction is subsequently remembered as a violent experience is comprehensible, because in this way the sense of guilt which otherwise would be devastating for the child is attenuated. A similar reaction occurs the first time by chance the parents are seen making love: the child who does not possess the categories which would make it possible to "read" that scene correctly immediately espouses the version of violence, the father's aggression toward the mother. In this way, too, the mother is freed of responsibility, rendering less bitter and intolerable her "betrayal."

We have said that Freud was the first psychotherapist to have had the courage to recognize emotional involvement with the patient; he was also the first to theorize on it. We have also said that Freud was, at least as much as those who preceded him, frightened by that involvement and thus tended to defend himself from it. Freud cleverly betrayed neither his quest for knowledge nor his need to defend himself, because his concept of transference allows the admission of the emotional involvement and, at the same time, its sterilization by means of its being both transformed into a therapeutic instrument and, more importantly, considered in some way "inauthentic." This inauthenticity is signalled by the choice of the term "transference," which implies diverting an emotional current from its normal destination and substituting it by means of a series of emotional messages to a false address (Szasz 1963; Chertok 1968). From this point of view, transference functions in the same way as Mesmer's magnetic fluid. Here as well the intent is to objectify therapeutic instruments and methods (Chertok 1968). Freud also obtained this result by pinpointing a factor external to the relationship as the origin of what occurred in the patient/therapist relationship. In Freud's case, the external factor is a third party, in both time and space, outside the field of the analytic relationship. The true recipient of the patient's affections is absent and has perhaps even disappeared into the past. The therapist is simply a stand-in for that recipient. Thus Freud was out of danger's way and could act within the analytic relationship as an observer, one who has no responsibility whatsoever for the emotional dynamics of the patient.

It is fortunate that things were put this way, at least in the beginning, because objectified transference not only served to reassure Freud, but also permitted his students to venture confidently out onto extremely treacherous ground. Mistaken or not, the conviction that it was possible to come out unscathed encouraged them to face their patients' emotional tempests without fear of dangerous consequences and made them somehow strong just where they were probably most vulnerable.

When Freud asked Jung's opinion on transference, Jung responded that it was analysis from A to Z. Freud concluded that Jung "had understood everything" and told him so (Jung 1961).

In fact, not only had Jung understood everything, he was destined not long afterward to understand it even more intensely, thanks to his affair with Sabina Spielrein. That "love that excuses no one loved from loving" succeeds in making its weight felt even within the analytic setting, where the love involved is transference love.

A simple interpretation, in such cases, is that the countertransference is the response to transference. The patient's love has not "excused" the analyst. The seduction set into action by the patient succeeds, despite the analyst's knowledge that he is not the true object of either the love or the seduction, but simply "in its path." His situation is similar to that of an actor in popular theater, who, playing the part of the villain, receives the invective and sometimes something more, inspired by the character he portrays.

Surely Freud, when a patient threw her arms around him, knew that such behavior had in fact nothing to do with him, as he did not consider himself particularly fascinating, but was directed at someone else, a phantasm with whom the patient had always had a rapport.

However, it is not unreasonable to ask whether we can be sure that Freud did nothing to foster those feelings, encourage the situation. Is the analyst really so totally innocent when such things occur?

Let us go back for a moment to what I have defined as the psychopathology of the analyst, that distant break in the ego–Self axis, caused by some lack in the primary object relationship, which leaves the adult with an open account to close, an emotional deficit to recover wherein no matter what he has he never has enough. In what attitudes, if not behavior, can that thirst for relationship which led him to choose psychotherapy as his profession be translated? What is the most ancient and least rudimentary tactic in that search for nourishment, the very particular nourishment which is the emotional relationship? Since the advent of humanity in the world, it has been seduction.

If love "moveth the earth and the firmament," then seduction moves love. Both the desired one and the feared one are seduced. Seduction is the most common method of relating to others and, all things considered, also the healthiest, if we compare it to annihilation, simple negation, or denial. Children seduce their parents; parents seduce their children. It is so closely interwoven a game that often it is difficult to distinguish action from reaction, initiative from response, and to judge correctly the complementary roles. We continue to define Don Juan as a gadabout, but there is a strong suspicion that it is the flower that seduces the bee. How often is the seducer actually induced to seduce and so, in the final analysis, seduced by his victim?

If Freud was insatiably hungry for affection and, further, had a so-called technical need of it as an instrument in the cure of his patient, is it really possible that he had done absolutely nothing to provoke what happened?

It goes without saying that we are not referring here to physical seduction, openly erotic seduction, given that the model is the ancient one of reciprocal seduction of mother and child in the primary relationship. We have already touched on parents and children. In fact, within couples, particularly young couples, there is a subtle struggle, often with no holds barred, to win the child's favor. It is a genuine contest as to which parent is the most seductive. And the child is made to order for seduction, not only as regards its little, round face and wide eyes. Its features, smiles, and captivating approaches as well are all programmed to inhibit adult aggression and arouse tenderness. But the relationship recalled in the analytic setting is the primary one, the most ancient uroboric rapport binding the child to the mother, and it is the psychological mechanisms characteristic of that relationship which are brought into play.

Freud maintained that the foundling makes the best patient; that is, the solitary person, the person without ties, who invests all his psychic energy in the analytic relationship, permitting the analyst to bind him to it (Rieff 1959, pp. 265–266). Consequently, Freud understood the necessity of "binding" the patient in the same way that mother and child reciprocally attempt to bind each other.

Nowadays, most analysts are perfectly aware that when patients throw their arms around them, it is exactly what the therapists wanted to happen, and exactly what they had subtly attempted to provoke. And yet it took considerable time for this reciprocity to be admitted. In fact, the concept of transference historically precedes the concept of countertransference. Evidently, it was more difficult for analysts to admit their own emotional involvement than that of their patients. The reason for this is that the admission subsequently, and perhaps even definitively, placed in jeopardy the "scientific nature" of their work.

All analysts should know, to the extent possible, what their own countertransference reactions might be and remain constantly aware of how they are experiencing the patient. Actually, their experience of the patient begins with the very first telephone conversation: the way in which the prospective patient proposes himself usually predisposes the analyst toward the patient in one way or another (Hillman 1972, p. 109).

It would be pointless to insist on deluding ourselves. The patient as an abstract entity does not, in reality, exist. Each patient is different, just as every therapist is different. And analysts inevitably end up orienting themselves toward a particular type of patient. It is true that the analyst's long training, making him familiar with his unconscious, should increase his relational capacity — the richer and more varied the pantheon of internal figures with which he has entered into clear and knowledgeable rapport, the wider the range of patients with whom he can tranquilly work. But the limits remain. There is always some part of the unconscious not sufficiently explored into which a patient can unexpectedly and unknowingly push, revealing problems which analysis did not succeed in bringing to the surface and which appear only at a particular moment in the therapy of a particular patient — in a situation which can be likened to the string of the *viola d'amore*, which vibrates spontaneously only when it resonates with a particular note.

Any analyst, after all, knows that his own analysis does not end when his training does, but is prolonged infinitely by his work with his patients, each of whom has the capacity to activate aspects in him still waiting to be analyzed and resolved. The most sensitive or difficult cases of involvement are usually those in which transference and countertransference emerge as love in a heterosexual patient–analyst couple. Love in the literal, universal, and unequivocal sense of the word, reciprocal passion recognized and in some way made explicit (Gorkin 1985). This obviously represents a quantum leap from the normal play of transference and countertransference. The seductive power of the patient in such cases is such that—to put it in the vernacular—the analyst is thrown from his horse.

Jung had such an experience in his relationship with Sabina Spielrein. In a beautiful letter, he wrote to his patient: "Remember when you were ill and I came to your aid. Now it is I who am unwell, and you must help me." The seduction had been so complete that it was Jung who could no longer do without his patient, in the same way a patient cannot cope without the analyst. The decision today to become an analyst is made in the full awareness that this work implies risks of this sort. The analyst must be fully aware that the emotions the patient develops regarding him are, in the end, activated by him (Hillman 1972, p. 120). This lucid awareness is a necessary condition (not, however, always sufficient) for the analyst to maintain control of the patient's feelings as well as his own, in order to utilize them solely for the purpose of therapy. It is not always sufficient because at times, as in Jung's case, the analyst can lose control in spite of his fundamental and underlying knowledge. This occurs most often when the heterosexual couple is made up of a male analyst and a female patient (Lester 1985; Goldberger and Evans 1985).

Why is it that a male analyst is more vulnerable when dealing with a female patient than a female analyst dealing with a male patient? Probably because the female child remains for a longer time in the maternal uroboric dimension resulting in a more intense training in the emotional sphere. The male analyst is constitutionally more vulnerable because he had to renounce precociously the uroboric dimension in order to differentiate himself from his mother. And in analysis, emotions are the operating currency.

Eleven

The Reciprocity of the Relationship

All human relationships are circular, and there is no reason to assume that the psychotherapist/patient relationship should be an exception. And yet today many analysts are still loath to admit the circularity of the psychoanalytic relationship, in the same way that people in general often persist in attributing to their partner exclusive responsibility for what happens in their relationships (Racker 1968).

The word "responsibility" should be sufficient to explain that resistance, that obstinate refusal to see. It is clear that awareness of the circularity of a relationship implies assuming most of the responsibility—not a very tempting prospect. The same culture that tends to make us responsible for events in the distant past (Adam's original sin, the Aztec genocide, slave trading, and colonialism, to name just a few) has, over the centuries, provided powerful antidotes canceling out more direct sorts of responsibility. Consequently, it is easier for us to admit having had a hand in the crucifixion of Christ than to admit our share of the responsibility in a disagreement with our partner.

The most obvious of antidotes, the most effective response to the necessity of finding an external persecutor upon whom we can place the entire responsibility for what happens to us, was the invention of the Devil, so external that when a possessed individual fought to keep it inside, an exorcist was given the task of driving it out. Even Jung, as we have seen, found it convenient to credit, not entirely in jest, some of his behavior of which he was not particularly proud, to the Devil, thus objectifying it to something external—that part of the Self which had led him into temptation.

It would be well to remember, however, that assuming an active role in a relationship also presents some positive aspects. Any analyst will have observed how a patient who has, for example, always been frustrated by emotional experience, once made aware of his own responsibility in interpersonal relationships, will unexpectedly reveal himself as capable of a totally different sort of relationship. The same person who had reaped only frustration and defeat was then able to experience emotional relationships calmly, obtaining gratification. Even meetings became "luckier," as if Destiny or some compassionate god had decided to reward him for his show of goodwill by letting him meet, at long last, the "right" person.

It is not heaven, chance, or lucky meetings that we are dealing with in such cases, however, so much as choice even if unwitting. It is inevitable that an individual who will not assume an active role in a relationship is unconsciously drawn to partners capable of oppressing and "castrating" him.

Something similar happens to in the analyst/patient relationship: even when the patient's choice of a particular analyst appears to have been the result of favorable circumstances, the selection was really guided unconsciously by the sort of expectations the patient has regarding psychotherapy, the result of which is the patient being drawn to the therapist who appears most promising in context of this hidden agenda. We are, of course, referring to deep and secret expectations, and not to those explicitly declared, in good faith possibly, but nonetheless inauthentic. A new patient will say and even believe that he wants to be freed of his neurosis, while actually nourishing the hope that he can learn to live with it. He will declare that he desperately needs to be emancipated, but secretly he is relishing the prospect of a new and reassuring dependence.

Thus the patient, whether he is aware of it or not, chooses his analyst in exactly the same way that the analyst chooses his patients. In short, every patient deserves the analyst he gets and vice versa. In *The Psychology of Transference*, Jung states that no one is able to carry another beyond one's own limits. If an analyst has still unviolated barriers, he will be able to lead his patient that far, and no further. Virgil conducted Dante to Hell and to Purgatory, but not to Paradise.

The qualifying element of an analyst's personality is the capacity to provoke in the patient a constellation of crucial emotional situations. That capacity, incidentally, cannot be created from nothing or provided by any training, because its existence depends on a human quality predating any training. But the patient as well, because of that same human quality, can present the analyst with crucial emotional situations. And the now famous story of Jung and Sabina Spielrein is proof of just that.

Jung's letters to Freud reveal a personality experiencing considerable difficulty on the emotional level, a sort of shutting off and defensiveness to that sphere of psychic life (Eissler 1982). Sabina Spielrein succeeded in opening a breach in those defenses, causing Jung to plunge headlong into an involved and disturbing emotional experience—an experience, however, from which he emerged richer.

Despite what we have said about certain qualities the analyst must possess even before embarking on training, we might mention that experience also plays an essential role in this profession. While it is possible to be a mature artist at age eighteen (in the so-called youthful production of Leopardi, there is already the entire range of the great poet in maturity) the analyst can elaborate upon the more hidden aspects of his personality only by accumulating experience in therapy.

We might go even further. Just as the patient derives vital energy from the analytic relationship, so the analyst is nourished by it. The concept of reciprocity returns and is completed. Every relationship, including analysis, whether we desire it or not, implies the beginning of a "double game." One gives if one receives and vice versa (Balint and Balint 1953, p. 66).

Within the analytical process, the first true problem to be faced is the confrontation of one's own repressed heterosexual dimension. In the process of sexual differentiation, we are led to identify totally not only with our sexual role but actually with a social stereotype: a woman is induced to repress the "male" in her, and a man the "female" in him. This, paradoxically, is a true "castration," as renouncing the development of our heterosexual counterpart means the automatic renouncing of the possibility of becoming psychologically whole. The integration of the opposite dimension of our sex, which we might call the dominating one, is extremely important, as the degree to which we are able to relate to the "woman" and, respectively, the "man" inside us, will determine the quality of our relationships with the woman or man outside us and the gratification derived from that meeting.

True contact with the interior heterosexual figure is far more essential for men, because women already naturally possess more developed relational capacities as a consequence of their having remained longer in the maternal matrix. Man is less "trained" in this area and is thus more likely to err. An obscure fear of placing his own sexual identity on the line induces him to repudiate and deny a large part of his own interior life and to suffocate at birth any "suspicious" impulses or needs which might prove dangerous to that uncertain identity. A woman, on the other hand, is able to experience without terror certain sensations and feelings seemingly not in keeping with her sexual role.

Even female homosexual experiences, we might add, are concerned above all with the sphere of emotion and express a need to recover a means of relating to the other which, too often, a woman fails to find with men, due to just that paradoxical castration.

But why is it that the female child remains longer than the male in the uroboric situation? There is certainly no need, in so early a phase, to hypothesize the existence of an "urge" or "natural imperative" to differentiate from the mother if the child is male, or conversely, the absence of such an urge if the child is female. It is enough to see in the child, particularly in this phase, a capacity to receive nonverbal messages from its mother. Thus, we could say that it is the mother who leads the game of differentiation or identification, partly knowingly and partly unknowingly. The mother begins very early (long before the well-known prohibitions, such as, "These are proper things for little boys" or "little girls," become explicit, heavily indicating all the "errors," at which point the uroboric phase should long have ended, at least theoretically) to see in her child the future little king, the little girl to be fondled, another version of herself who will have everything she didn't, or the future "little man," who will grow up the way she would like him to because he is the Prince Charming who comes from afar, even if in so small an edition, a rosebud.

The mother presents herself to her male child in a differentiated way, when she speaks to him, when she rocks him to sleep, when she tells him about his future, when she plays with him, even when she daydreams. It would not be rash to suppose that when this differentiated attitude is lacking, eliciting, for example, an identification with the mother in the little boy, it is quite probable that he will have some difficulty in orienting himself sexually later on. Certainly I do not claim that the heart of the problem of homosexuality is here. However, it is not completely unreasonable to trace to this early phase the origins of at least one aspect of that vast and variegated phenomenon: the difficulty or impossibility of identifying with one's own physiological sex, which is a possible premise for later tendencies and compulsive choices.

To conclude, if the female child experiences identification with the mother, and the male child experiences otherness, the length of time in the maternal nest will not represent any threat to the female child's identity, while the male child will feel the vague urge to differentiate. It is here that we find the origins of an insufficient relational capacity in the adult male. In fleeing from the mother, he also turns his back on the possibility of deeply assimilating the relational dimension (Neumann 1959, p. 66). We might even hypothesize that the need to objectify, typical of the scientific world, is more relevant to the male condition due to that particular aspect of psychological development.

What matters, however, is to avoid confusing cultural data with "natural" data, considering "male" and "female" as purely and simply sexual connotations, the designation of which must scrupulously follow the established dividing line between the two "registered" sexes, instead of considering them as human qualities and attitudes which each one of us has and which must be allowed to develop.

It is paradoxical that it should be in the human species, which does not possess a very marked sexual dimorphism, that culture has succeeded in creating a considerably greater psychic dimorphism, in which man and woman, although part of the same ecosystem and thus forced to accept compromise, complicity, and reciprocal dependency, seem to belong to totally different worlds — mutually inaccessible and foreign.

I am convinced that humanity is moving toward a new culture, in which that patrimony which has been roughly divided up and parceled out to the two sexes will become once again available to all. I do not invoke here the myth of the hermaphrodite; I am simply advocating an end to having half of one's potential personality amputated.

I am also convinced that it is not true that there is nothing to do but wait patiently for that advent, at most making predictions whenever possible and proselytizing. Psychologists have the right and the duty to suppose that from this point on it will be possible for the individual to escape cultural subjugation. It is a matter of life and death for them, or in any case, for their profession. If every individual were perfectly molded by culture or society, psychology would not exist. There would be only sociology.

The psychologist, obviously, cannot avoid starting out with the conviction that for the individual it is possible to respond autonomously to cultural and social pressures which, although they have certainly conditioned him from birth and before birth, since they conditioned his parents as well, have not lobotomized him. For the psychologist-analyst, this basic conviction is transformed into the thankless task of pushing the patient toward a painful acceptance of responsibility, painful because it calls into question the simplest and most efficient of alibis for his weaknesses and defeats.

Man's need to find a scapegoat goes back to the origins of the species and consequently is a primitive need: projection as a defense mechanism is, in psychological terms, the most infantile in the relation to reality. Progressively, as we mature, we must learn to understand that the most fearsome enemy is within us, is part of us. As long as we feel bombarded and harassed by others, by fate, or by the rest of the world, we will surely not be in a position to take our fate into our own hands. This does not, of course, mean that it is healthy to assume the blame for all of society's ills or to assert that there are no charlatans in the world, no "power-hungry" oppressors who, having failed to master themselves, aim at mastering others. The analyst knows well enough that these others are not just projections of the worst side of ourselves; they do in fact exist and have their own projects to be pursued and realized, and it is possible that some of those projects are objectively hostile, harmful, and unjust. But as the analyst knows, a patient who has gone into analysis seeing himself as a target, threatened by all, must first clear the air of so abnormal a view of things, postponing to a later phase the finer adjustments which may be required.

Jungian metapsychology provides us with quite another strategy for enlarging upon the significance of our suffering and our problems. Instead of attributing responsibility for them to the rest of the world in order to relieve ourselves of that responsibility, we put them back into the context of the history of all mankind, which each one of us relives in our individual history. In this way, it is possible to escape the sense of the absurd, making of every human life a project and a plan for realizing it. What usually is possible only in retrospect—the perception of a clear pattern in events that at the time seemed casual and without particular sense, the way that moving away from a painting blurs the details but clarifies the meaning of the whole—can also be possible at every moment. But this is only possible if we accept once again the responsibility for what happens to us, because we never will succeed in making sense of the mysterious plots of others or blows indiscriminately dealt by Chance. The more we refuse to accept responsibility for our defeats, the more we effectively delegate the control of our destiny to others, because that victim's attitude supposes us to be, and renders us, unarmed before reality. Only if we feel responsible will we also feel free, regardless of the force of pressures and conditioning besetting us.

The Jungian view also suggests how we can ward off another paralyzing danger, another false enemy, the past experienced in a determinist perspective. Our destiny is not written down in the past. Our personal history conditions us, but no more than the external world does. We must feel free also of our past. It is impossible to deny or negate it, but it is absurd to confuse it with our future. It is inside us, a part of us, and as such we have to deal with it, learn to understand it, but we must not be swept away or crushed by it, for although our past is a part of us, it is not all of us. We are, after all, children of our past. And the true destiny of children is to become independent.

Twelve

Neutral Permeability

The expression "transference neurosis" has two meanings. First it is the category of neurosis that Freud distinguishes from narcissistic neurosis by virtue of the fact that transference neurosis is a psychological disorder treatable by analysis because in analysis the patient is capable of object investments—whether real or imaginary—which permit the formation of a transference relationship with the analyst in the place of the original figure.

Its second meaning is the artificial neurosis in which symptoms of transference tend to develop: those emotional phenomena that emerge within the analytical relationship and appear to displace the patient's real motives for going into analysis. In effect, the analysis itself becomes the problem.

It is as though the transference neurosis substitutes for an older neurosis with the resulting advantage, however, that this time the analyst directly witnesses the evolution of the process. He is directly involved in the repetition compulsion of the other and thus participates in that artificial disorder, "contaminating" positively also the neurotic aspects and suffering that led the patient to seek therapy.

In working through the transference, the nucleus of the neurosis is dissolved as, within the analytic relationship, the essential points of the patient's suffering mysteriously come together.

In the course of our historical digression on the object relationship between therapist and patient, we suggested that in introducing the concept of transference, Freud actually remained more or less consistent with the defensive line taken by his predecessors—that need to neutralize and sterilize the relationship which led Mesmer to attribute to the magnetic fluid the responsibility for the phenomena he observed (Chertok and De Saussure 1973).

The first Freudian definition of transference saw it as a "false link" (Freud 1895, p. 438). That is, the analyst was bestowed affection through a mechanism of inexact connections between his own figure and the desires of the patient. Later, in *Fragment of an Analysis of a Case of Hysteria* (1901), which refers to the famous clinical case of Dora, Freud would state that transference is nothing more than a "newer edition" of something very old. The analytic situation permits a reliving of a complex emotional situation, the first setting for which is found in the patient's past. Nowadays, this is the "orthodox" position. In it, the analyst restores the patient's emotional content, because according to this view, it is not the analyst who is the real object of that investment. His presence in the patient's psychological field permits the reactivation of old emotional situations for which the analyst functions as support. He works together with the patient on the emotional material that emerges, in the full knowledge that it does not belong to him. Revision and false connection would appear then to be two essential aspects of the Freudian concept of transference.

However, in order to fully understand Freud's view, it is necessary to look at his theories on transference in the context of the repetition compulsion, presented in *Beyond the Pleasure Principle* (Freud 1920), in which is given the final modification of the theory of drives: the antagonism between the life drive and the death drive. According to this concept, there exists in people, as in all living things, a tendency to return to the "state of inorganic stability" (ibid., pp. 36–39). On the psychological level, this tendency is expressed in the unconscious mechanism—otherwise inexplicable exclusively in light of the pleasure principle—of a compulsion to repeat old, repressed, and painful experiences.

Freudian speculation on the death instinct demonstrates once again the repetitive aspects of the transference phenomenon as the tendency of the repressed conflict to present a newer version of itself in the relationship with the analyst (Laplanche-Pontalis 1967, p. 41). Thus, in its classic definition, transference represents a theoretical instrument that permits the analyst to defend himself from the patient's attempts to involve him directly and allows him to consider himself as nothing more than a lucid witness to the patient's confrontation with old specters.

Subsequently, and above all thanks to Jung and existential psychoanalysis, the analytic relationship took on new meaning with the "discovery" of countertransference. Less perceptive analysts believe that countertransference is an emotional reaction to the patient's transference. The truth is, however, that the analyst and the patient contribute equally and simultaneously to create the emotional field of the relationship to the degree that it might be more precise to refer to the transference of the patient and the transference of the analyst (Brenner 1976).

In the glory days of psychoanalysis, physicians procured analytical training in fairly short order. They read the writings of Freud, rushed off to Vienna for a week of analysis, and went back home, ready to hang out their shingle. It was not long before it became clear that if the microscope was not clean, the dirty lens would hinder observation. Metaphor aside, the fact that the analyst was not aware of his own emotional complexes constituted a serious impediment to his understanding of the patient's. It was the Zurich school which first recommended — and later made obligatory — full analytic treatment for anyone thinking of taking up the profession. This training consisted of what was modestly called "didactic analysis," in an ingenuous attempt to make a distinction between those in treatment for neurotic disturbances and those who entered analysis solely for the purpose of curing them. In reality, the difference is not at all that great, because each request to become an analyst is more or less an unconscious request for therapeutic treatment.

What are the selection criteria for admission to the various psychoanalytic associations? Naturally, in the interview with the didactic analyst, it is not the candidate's theoretical mastery which is evaluated, even though the cultural level of the therapist is extremely important in our work. Instead, it is on the psychological disturbances of the aspiring analyst that attention is centered. The didactic analyst looks for them and is delighted if he finds them, because it is precisely those aspects of the personality which are transformed into true analytical instruments. The didactic analyst knows that the unhealed wound is the opening through which the future therapist will be able to delve into his own unconscious. Only from this point of view is the difference between didactic analysis and "normal" analysis actually of any consequence. The training, rather than curing the future analyst, acts to make him aware of his own disturbances; such awareness of these fractures, these "weaknesses," can be transformed into great strength. If we are aware of the more problematic facets of our personality, we are also aware of where we might fail and where we might succeed. Every time the analyst begins a relationship with a new patient, his unconscious is reactivated. However, if he is aware of his own weak spots, he will be able to move more effectively within the delicate processes of the psyche. The first analytical experiences are always very difficult, precisely because they require considerable personal involvement, and there exist no individual or didactic analyses that penetrate as deeply as the analytic relationship with the patient.

The analyst is thus always in analysis, not so much because he has his own analyst to lean on, but because the relationship with the patient stimulates in him crucial questions. The mirror-analyst by now belongs to the prehistory of psychoanalysis. The new type of analyst does not expect the patient's suffering to bounce off him like a ball against the cushions of the billiard table; he is neither so compact nor so impervious. And if, at times, he appears inattentive, it is because his is a fluctuating attention, not listening to the patient because he is listening attentively to his own inner reactions. There are those who wonder whether or not the analyst should mention his countertransference to the patient. However, this is a moot point; in a relationship as intimate as that of patient and analyst, even without speaking, one is fully aware of the state of mind of the other (Tauber 1954, Berman 1949). In fact, a slightly sadistic patient will do his utmost to torment by continually bringing up the sort of subject he senses is painful for the analyst. There are patients who relate only bad news, others who cleverly alternate the good with the bad, and still others who are eternal Spring. It is certain, in any case, that the inner dimension of the analyst is understood very well by the analysand.

The origin of this reciprocal permeability of patient and analyst can probably be found in the uroboric mother–child model, in which for a long period the only interpersonal exchange is nonverbal. This pattern, as common experience proves, can be reactivated at any moment of our adult life, whenever we are truly involved in an ultimate relationship.

As happens often enough, we risk passing from the analyst's energetic insistence on his own neutrality to the opposite extreme. The gradual acceptance and awareness, first of the analyst's involvement (thanks to transference) and then of the reciprocity of the emotional and affective currents (thanks to countertransference), recently induced some excessively sensitive—or insensitive—souls to advance the theory of a sort of parity of analyst and patient within the therapeutic setting. This is blatant demagoguery and clearly unfounded (Rieff 1959, p. 264). I well realize that a subtle reader might suspect that my words could be hiding—and might reveal—in exactly the same way as Mesmer's magnetic fluid, a need to defend—no longer the neutrality and calm detachment of the therapist, but at any rate, that last vestige of privilege left him to defend—"charisma." But I cannot resist mentioning that not only do completely equal interpersonal relationships not exist, but the psychotherapeutic relationship in particular is based from the outset on an asymmetry that could be defined as structural. The nature of the patient's projections onto the analyst and the regressiveness of those projections imply unequivocally a clear-cut inequality. However, the attribution of power, which occurs the moment we turn to someone for help, already suffices to throw the relationship off balance. This does not, however, exclude a psychological exchange between analyst and patient, even if from different and asymmetrical positions.

We have said that choosing the profession of psychoanalysis is motivated by distant, very early emotional situations, because it is in infancy that certain tendencies emerge, influencing the life of the adult in certain ways. Unsatisfactory early object relationships subsequently induce the adult to continuously repropose relationships to himself through the well-known mechanism of repetition compulsion.

Perhaps I should specify that I use this term in a somewhat different context than the orthodox Freudian one, thus severing from it the self-destructive implications connected with the death drive, upon which even Freudians are careful not to insist without first expressing explicit reservations. We know how fascinated Freud was by double schemas, and in his metapsychology, an equal and contrary instinct to the life or Eros instinct was the "missing link" in the conflict between the self, the ego, and the superego.

Regarding this I should like to digress slightly. It is clear that if the Freudians themselves question the death instinct, it is not up to us to

make theoretical objections, which in any case were already antici-
pated by Freud when he realized that: "since the assumption of the
existence of the instinct is mainly based on theoretical grounds, we
must also admit that it is not entirely proof against theoretical objections" (Freud 1927–1931, pp. 121–122). More relevant to our inquiry
into the analyst's secret, personal motivations, both as to choice of
profession and theoretical formulations, would be to reflect a bit on
the notion itself. One often hears about "the influence of Schopenhauer." Influences, however, are seeds which flourish only in
fertile ground predisposed to receive them.

Why did Freud consider it so right and necessary to institutionalize
a self-destructive instinct as a counter to the life instinct? Very qualified analysts have argued that an aggressive instinct "perversely"
directed toward the self would have been sufficient to explain the
compulsion to repeat negative, or self-destructive, experiences. Perhaps it was not an entirely rational matter. Darkness as a quality in
itself and not as the absence of light, death as a condition apart and
not merely the absence of life, are misunderstandings as old as
humankind, and for this reason they must remain the prerogative of
poets and children. The poet has desperate need of metaphor, the
child of somehow ordering a contradictory and incomprehensible
reality, thus interpreting the absence of the mother as the presence of
a bad (not available) mother.

Filling a void with a negative fantasy is the simplest form of exorcism. Even the Christian Church, which shook off all Manichaean
heresy with its stunning intuition of evil as the absence of good,
continued on unperturbed, making evil concrete (the Devil, Hell)
and conferring on it eternal life. And yet, if we look carefully at many
of our linguistic "tics," we see just how often opposites are not two
entities, but two degrees of the same thing. Certainly, love and hate
are true opposites. The absence of love is not hate, and it is not
enough to stop hating someone in order to be able to say we love
them. But what about strength and weakness? What is weakness if
not the lack or want of strength? And might we not say the same of
knowledge and ignorance, certainty and uncertainty, and so many
other pairs of concepts in which one element defines a quality, while
the other is limited to indicating its *absence*? Thus, when a vital
instinct is postulated, it should not be necessary to postulate another,
equal and contrary, to it. It would be enough to run out of the first

101

for everything to die out and dry up, "returning to the inorganic state."

Incidentally, ethologists have found only one example—and an extremely rare one at that—of something which might indicate that *homo sapiens* is not the only species with this extra "instinct": the collective suicide of certain animals when their habitat becomes impracticable. But we are dealing here with a suicide that is collective and its cause objective. Even in this case, the hypothesis advanced is that something ceases to function, and something else comes into play. In the case of the jungle cat, which in captivity lets itself die of starvation, it is enough that a vital instinct is snuffed out, the instinct to nourish itself. What need is there to postulate an equal or contrary instinct?

It would appear that there were no serious objective theoretical reasons for Freud to substantiate the shadows or hypothesize an adversary to the will to live, especially since he himself theorized that an impulse—amorous or aggressive—normally directed outward could function as a boomerang. In an attempt to understand what might have led Freud to excogitate—and maintain energetically till the end—this postulate, it might be helpful here to refer to two hypotheses dear to my heart. The first is that every metapsychology carries the stigmata of its creator, and the second is that the secret motive behind every attempt to objectify psychic phenomena is the necessity to defend against and eliminate responsibility. From what could a man like Freud need to defend himself, weighed down as he was by a superego as big as a mountain? For such a man, giving substance to shadows is the only hope of salvation. Not only must destructivity be objectified as an entity in itself, not only must it be attributed to a constitutional factor (thus freeing the creature from responsibility and casting suspicion on the Creator); but it must be directed against the self and only partially diverted outwards, instead of the other way around.

Returning to our discussion of repetition compulsion in choice of profession, all those who practice professions wherein the human relationship is the raw material have probably experienced a break in the ego–self axis and consequently also the profound desire to "reduce," using a surgical term, this break. The analyst's profession above all others perhaps most adheres to this primitive need, as it is set within the framework of a deep emotional relationship. In analysis, what are evoked are not forgotten memories (that is a paleolithic concept of psychoanalysis). What are actually repressed are emotions, or sensations, related to the events. For example, anger experienced by a child toward its parents may be repressed if it becomes harmful when acted out. In analysis, it is just this sort of repressed emotion which emerges, even if the reality of the current situation does not justify the patient's emotional state. If there have been profound wounds inflicted on the child in its emotional life, if its relationships with significant persons have been difficult to downright disastrous, then throughout its entire existence there will be an unconscious tendency to repropose the same painful experiences, in the attempt to overcome them.

It should be clear in what sense we have used the term repetition compulsion without the negative connotations attributed to it by Freud. It is obvious that a repetition compulsion characterized by the more or less unconscious intent to get over, by dint of trying again and again, the obstacle which once got the better of us, paralyzing or mortally wounding us, is no longer destructive but, on the contrary, constructive. The difference between the two concepts is radical; they are poles apart. The immediate results can sometimes be the same, for if one persists in measuring oneself against an adversary that has proven itself superior, one risks extreme consequences. However, it is one thing to ask for a return match and quite another to want the humiliation of defeat.

Our concept is comparable to Adler's "handicap challenge": the inferiority complex induces us to excel in precisely that area where we feel inferior. I hasten to add, however, that this original handicap does not coincide at all with an original defect, which would diminish in some way the authenticity and value of choosing this profession, just as the Freudian interpretation of artistic creativity as the sublimation of libidinous energy does not devalue the vocation or the talent of the artist, the noble aspirations of his work, or the intrinsic, objective value of his art. However, coming back to the analyst, reacting to a handicap with a challenge and, in particular this challenge, is not an automatic compulsive response, but a choice. We know well how many other forms the search for a return match can take. One example is a form at the expense of others. What is important is the analyst's awareness of the deep need to which his choice was intended to respond. It is this basic awareness that permits him to experience appropriately the inner resonances stimulated in him by his patients and to confidently trust his own capacity to enter into an empathic relationship with them—a capacity that is no longer mysterious or disturbing once its origins are known.

In the light of that awareness, even the concept of countertransference appears a profoundly different one than that described in the manuals as influences exerted by the patient on the analyst's unconscious. In this clearer view, countertransference is the entire psychological world of the analyst, which is continually activated within a relationship we might define (borrowing a term from theologian and religious historian, Martin Buber) as the "I–thou" sort. This is the authentic interpersonal relationship between two subjects with which Buber opposes the I–He relation wherein the other is object (Buber 1954, pp. 9–35). That old interior laceration, that break in the ego–Self axis, that perpetually unhealed wound permitting the analyst to look through a small opening deep into himself, also permits him to participate in his relationship with the patient with his entire self, including the deepest layers. But so authentic, complete, and defenseless a relationship must inevitably imply vulnerability for the analyst, who is exposed no less than the patient to what Jung called "psychic infection" (1946, pp. 176–177).

From different positions, both patient and analyst are assailable, exposed to contagion. If the analyst "contaminates" the patient by entering the patient's inner world, at the same time opening the door to his own, the patient will do the same. It is not unidirectional, a blood transfusion in which there is a donor and a recipient, but a singular reciprocal transfusion, in which (to extend the metaphor) the ideal analyst would have blood type O, and thus be a universal donor, capable of operating with the widest possible range of patients.

This reciprocal contagion can cause phenomena that might appear abnormal, but which are actually full-fledged elements of the analytic process. The most obvious, most sensational, and most disturbing for all concerned—from the patient and his entourage to the analyst—is what Freud would call "transference love" (Freud 1914).

We have already touched on the defensive function implicit in this term, which suggests the idea of love going astray. The defense to which we alluded then regarded the secret need of the therapist to prevent his work from being disturbed by emotional involvement.

We might point out another defensive function, more prosaic and more literal, that of protecting the psychoanalyst from being accused of manipulating the affective and erotic sentiments of the patient. The concept of transference love served very well to defend the analyst on two fronts, the interior and the exterior (Chertok 1968).

The accusations leveled at the psychoanalysts were remarkably similar to those that have been leveled since the beginning of dynamic psychiatry. Remember that a century and a half earlier, the inquiry conducted by the French Academy on Mesmer's magnetism produced two sets of results, one public and one private. It was only in the private version that the sexual implications of that therapeutic practice were mentioned. Official Western culture, as we know, has always demonstrated an exceptional sensitivity as regards this problem and the extraordinary olfactory sense of a specially trained bloodhound in sniffing out its presence. Freud was very well aware of this and indicated that the richest source of pathogenic conflicts could be found in sexual repression, an aspect of life which in Judeo-Christian tradition was branded as sin, if not sin *par excellence*,

Even today, transference love, although it no longer gives rise to scandal, at the very least provokes irony and scorn in laypeople, not only those less cultured, but intellectuals as well—Philip Roth, for example, and film director Woody Allen, two names taken directly from the Parnassus of American narrative and cinema, in a country where psychoanalysts's studios are more frequented than gymnasium and dancing schools.

Yet, the truly thorny cases, those which have caused so many of the accusations made against psychoanalysts like Mesmer, are not truly representative. On a bell curve, they would be situated on the extreme edges, where the frequency of error is very slight as compared to the mean. But the exception is, as we well know, often more spectacular and newsworthy than the rule. If it were not, there would be no adage about one rotten apple spoiling the lot.

Thirteen

Love and the Relationship

If, as we have said, the feelings involved in analysis are authentic and not simply the result of misunderstanding or error, in what way does the analytic relationship differ from a routine, normal couple relationship?

The answer to this lies not so much in the fact that it has been programmed (for matrimony, an obvious example, is programmed as well, at least theoretically, as regards the intentions of the contracting parties, law, and tradition) as in its experimental nature. Because one of the partners is, in fact, experimenting with the relationship—in spite of the fact that he is in it up to his neck, which renders his task extremely difficult. The analytic relationship is not a simulation in the sense of an aeronautic simulation, in which pilots are trained in aircraft where actual flight conditions are simulated, but rather an experimental situation in the classic sense; that is, the real characteristics of a phenomenon are concentrated, focused upon, and intensified, utilizing certain insights, so that the entire cycle is completed in a shorter period of time. The experiment functions somewhat like a magnifying lens which can concentrate the rays of the sun upon a particular point to generate intense heat. In this sense, the transference experience exemplifies the affective pull experienced in any relationship, with the exception that it is concentrated, illuminated, magnified.

We must not forget that in the psychic life the relationship is of vital importance. In fact, there has always been the concept of punishment as isolation or segregation, the most relevant aspect of which is not the reduction of the individual to impotence, but being denied relationship with the external world. We know that, although the reasons for going into analysis are varied, one of the principal ones is inevitably frustration of the capacity to relate, usually formed during the first object relationship with the parents. This basic experience is transmitted as an imprinting which lasts throughout our entire existence. Although in many religions, Christianity included, preference is given to the relationship with the divinity — the relationship with one's fellows being a mere reflection of that all-important one — and although the mystics of those religions actually consider voluntary isolation (the holy recluse, the buried alive) the ideal condition for relating to God, solitude remains the greatest of human suffering. Of course, lack of relationships is borne in various ways, depending on the age and psychological history of each individual. For example, an aged person may succeed in doing without real relationships if throughout his earlier existence he was nourished by a deep relationship. For the young, however, the prospect of spending one's entire life alone is truly a painful one. Relationship with the other is also exceptionally stimulating: we all know what tremendous energy flows from a successful relationship and what we are capable of doing with that energy.

But let us go back to the analytic relationship. We cannot say that transference is a characteristic exclusive to the analytic relationship for the very good reason that no relationship exists in which transference does not play a fundamental role. All our encounters assume the shape and form of the models of our first object relationships and are fraught with the same significance. However, this does not mean that our adult relationships are inauthentic, but simply that they originate in infantile desires directed toward important persons — urgent, pressing, and insatiable desires which were never entirely satisfied. For this reason, our object choices continue to be directed toward figures similar to those earlier ones with whom we wish to settle a score.

This is why in analysis the initial situation is a regressive one, unequal, since it usually involves one who receives and another who gives; one weaker and the other stronger. But in this case, that strength is also, if not exclusively, the knowledge of certain psychological mechanisms. It is upon this strength that the analyst must build in order to bring about his patient's cure by stimulating him to grow.

The possibility of psychological development is always the result of a confrontation with our most secret psychic contents, which during the process of education were expunged from our consciousness because they were considered negative. Becoming conscious of those contents is essential to the total recovery of the personality. This process is very painful, as it compels us to confront all those parts of ourselves we prefer to look away from, actually forgetting them. Doing otherwise would mean questioning a process that appeared to have totally succeeded: the remodeling of our personality, eliminating anything which did not fit the new image.

A superstructure, certainly — practically a prosthesis — or what Jung called the persona, has long enabled us to function without feelings of shame, and it is not easy to discard, as one might get rid of an article of clothing or a mask. It has grown with us, gradually adhering to us and becoming one with our skin. Attempting to tear it off would cause strips of our flesh to come away with it in the process.

This sort of plastic surgery has never been entirely successful. It only succeeds in disguising certain defects. Our apparent personality can do no more than conceal certain weaknesses, which taken all together constitute what Jung called the shadow and Freud "painful, repressed content," and which is nothing more or less than the unconscious. The proof that the operation only partially succeeds lies in the fact that this repressed psychic content can emerge in a disguised form, symptoms. But even when it does not get that far, it can still make its presence felt by causing us to experience sensations of discontent and pain.

When, at the beginning of the analysis, the patient finds himself having to confront these unrewarding and negative aspects of his own personality, the analyst can expect some instinctive reaction, like the hand that recoils from a burning or repugnant object. The therapist must confront this resistance from the very beginning of the analysis, not by demolishing it but by working with it.

The analyst also works with the transference, and this does not constitute a contradiction, since transference is nothing more than one of those reactions, one of those instinctive responses. Such resistances can be of various types, ranging from actual flight to severe withdrawal. However, the most frequent response is transference, which takes different forms, as we shall see further on. But transference love is also a means — perhaps the most sophisticated one, and the most cleverly disguised—of resisting the analysis. While appearing to be running toward the analyst with arms open wide, the patient is actually changing the subject, changing the meaning of the words, switching games, with the secret and unconscious intent of postponing indefinitely the game begun, which has not been going his way. Falling in love as a means of defense is a well-known phenomenon outside the analytic setting also. The subtle, unconscious calculations underlying love are what many such choices are based on; such love would otherwise be inexplicable. In the very much discussed phenomenon of "love of the enemy" (from the impressive number of cases recorded of amorous collaboration during the Second World War, to the more recent Stockholm Syndrome) other factors, both subjective and objective, are also involved.

It is pointless to discuss the authenticity of the feelings characterizing the transference, both because all feelings are transference and because in the final analysis a feeling is, if experienced and not pretended, automatically authentic. However, one might ask, in light of these observations on the patient's unconsciously pursued ends, whether transference love is useful to the analysis or damaging to it, even irreparably.

That love, having established that it is actually love, should have its own ends should not shock us. All passion can and must proceed to its own conclusion, since its authentic destination is in external reality and not only in our inner theater. Let us consider then what other characteristic of love, unqualified love, can alarm (and understandably so) the therapist.

The analytic relationship is based on an unwritten, if explicit, agreement. After an initial trial period, the analyst reestablishes the relationship by saying to the patient that they will continue on together and that, no matter what happens, the relationship will not be broken off. He says this because he knows that sooner or later the resistances will intervene, that inevitably unpleasant, even painful, psychic content will emerge, and just as inevitably the patient will attempt to block it by attacking directly the one activating the process—the analyst. That attack can be made in various ways; a vast array of cases have been documented, ranging from the most violent hatred to the most tender seduction. Of all the strategies possible, transference love is undoubtedly the most alarming to the therapist; at the very least, it is the one most difficult for him to control, because in a person who loves, the rational faculties are impaired. Should the analyst, in order to defend himself, attempt to reason with the patient, he will have difficulty knowing just where to begin. Fortunately, love heeds neither advice nor adversity.

Why fortunately? Because the salvation of the analyst—and the success of the therapy—lies not in self-defense, but in experiencing fully the trials, risks, and mystery of that passionate involvement. An analyst worthy of the name, up to his task, when faced with this challenge does not feel lost nor does he opt for surrender or flight. Instead, he accepts the challenge on the patient's terms; he accepts the struggle with the demon love.

At this point, our focus shifts again to the personality of the analyst, who must by no means be "above" passion. In fact, we might even go so far as to say that his strength actually lies in his weakness. He was not, like Achilles, immersed in childhood into the river Styx in order to be made invulnerable, but into a flow of emotions and affection that instead rendered him more vulnerable, precisely in those areas of ablution. The Achilles heel of the analyst is the whole sphere of feelings, because that singular baptism kindled in him an insatiable need to go on endlessly trying his strength against the demon of the unconscious—not unlike the duelists of Ridley Scott. The true analyst is not a sage who has come up with all the calming, reassuring answers, but a troubled, restless spirit, forever in search of the more complete answer, which at any rate is not in the offing because what he actually seeks is nothing less than the meaning of life. And a lifetime will not suffice to find it; that is, without embracing ready-made solutions or certain dogmas.

The challenge for the analyst is the emotional relationship. Consequently, his inner demon is evoked, provoked, and aroused only in interpersonal relationships and only when the other enters into it. Thus, transference love as a resistance of the patient is closely bound up with the personality of the therapist. The patient does not fall in love only because he finds himself in difficulty within the analysis, but also because the analyst, in an attempt to activate the patient's own inner demon and to render the patient capable of facing a frustrating reality, is playing with fire; that is, in the attempt to strike a spark, the analyst runs the serious risk of kindling a bonfire.

It is clear that by falling in love with the analyst, the patient is turning the tables on him. It is as though the patient would delegate to the analyst and the analyst's inner demon, which he senses as alive and strong, the struggle for liberation, the difficult choices and dangerous decisions. But this is not the agreement; the analyst's job is to help the patient find within himself both the energy and the capacity to use it to grow autonomously.

If then the analyst is playing with fire, we can only hope that he is not an incompetent like the well-known sorcerer's apprentice, even if one basically never stops learning, for we are all apprentices for life. We might say that the analyst handles explosives, plays with dynamite, his job being to make it explode, but come out intact. Failing this, any patient might be his last.

But, I repeat, transference love is not an artificial emotion nor is it a surrogate, and, generally speaking, transference is not a phenomenon exclusive to the analytic relationship. The therapist's need to protect himself from awkward involvements is the main reason why this concept took so long to be verified and accepted. In fact, today there are still those who question its validity. Obviously, the therapist still is—as he was two centuries ago—unable to overcome his secret fear of the relationship with the patient, continuing to place between himself and that patient some magnetic fluid, some reassuring, sterile definition of the impetuous emotions the patient transmits to him.

Turning from the therapist's need to defend himself to the need to defend the therapy from the patient's rash attacks, the issues become more complicated. What the therapist experiences is not, unfortunately, totally lacking in ambiguity; it is complex and contradictory, especially the experience of transference love. Any analyst knows how often love is used to destroy the analysis, but he also knows that equally often it encourages progress.

Having established the fact that the love and hate circulating within the analytic setting are real and do not differ in the slightest way from their counterparts outside it, analysis can thus be considered a model of human relationship, with all the games of projection and counter-projection which characterize it. Transference love can be considered a model of the love relationship, even if initially the tacit agreement between analyst and patient introduces an element not always present in situations outside the therapeutic setting: the prohibition of going beyond the limits of a verbal relationship. Often not always, even in a normal love relationship, there are from the outset analogous prohibitions of a social, class, or individual origin—prior commitments, subjective inhibitions, and insuperable obstacles. But all pacts, as we know, are made to be broken.

The pact stipulated between analyst and patient provides that the patient pay a set amount of money for a certain number of hours of the analyst's time each week, and the tacit, sometimes even explicit, understanding is that the relationship will grow, as it were, at a safe distance—that is, through verbal expression. This means that at the beginning of the relationship, both parties are aware of the premises upon which their relationship is based and thus, the patient (male or female) knows, or believes he knows, the limits within which events will proceed.

Subsequently, however, the patient will realize, either gradually or all at once, that something is changing or already has changed. He will realize that his experience no longer has anything to do with the initial assumptions of the therapy. This is what Freud called the transference neurosis. The theme, the object, of analysis is no longer the problem that originally brought the patient into therapy; rather a new problem actually forms within the setting, a new disorder or symptom. The treatment has become in its turn the illness to be treated—an interesting paradox, which in theory could begin an endless game of boxes within boxes, but which in reality means that the problem, remaining what it was, has been essentially recreated within the analytic setting where it is easier to "analyze" because it is present both in its current as well as its formative phase.

If this is not the situation, then the analysis has not yet begun. If, between the analyst and the patient, everything flows smoothly without problems, it means that the game has not yet got under way, that we are still in the preliminary stage, where—as in boxing—each of the two contenders sizes the other up and tests, not so much the intentions of the adversary as his actual substance and complexity, so as to understand his reactions and of what stuff the other is actually made.

Obviously, in this cat-and-mouse game, the analyst is the cat. Even if the patient moves with caution, he is on unfamiliar ground, riddled with mysterious traps. The analyst, on the other hand, is on his own home ground, lying in wait, tranquil and sly, biding his time, even feigning catlike indifference. He never loses sight of his "victim," who will surely sooner or later fall into his trap.

The patient, intrigued by this Sphinx-like presence, at first feels compelled to try and decipher it, examine it, investigate it in order to explain its charismatic power. Either he does not realize or else cannot accept the explanation that for the most part he himself delegated that power to the analyst the moment he chose him as his savior, and that the analyst's charisma, quite apart from any real individual qualities, is his automatically, by virtue of his position. When the patient's interest becomes dominant and exclusive, the transference has begun: the therapist has become the center of the patient's emotional and affective life.

Transference is an essential part of therapy, both because it recreates the model of an emotional event particular to each patient, in an ideal setting, and because it is only by living out an emotional storm that the patient in analysis — and, incidentally, also anyone outside the setting — finally sheds his masks and disguises and discovers himself. It is above all in transference love that the patient reveals himself for what he is and not for what he would like to be or thinks he is (which is what occurs in any case when one falls in love). It is at this point only that the analyst truly knows his patient because it is only by falling in love that an individual's true face is revealed, indicating the correct course of a human affair.

In amore veritas. But here we have the reverse of this well-known commonplace according to which love renders us unrecognizable, temporarily different, deprived of our real personality. The truth is that never are we so authentic. If love has made us another person, it means that we always were that other person, even if we never let on. It is not love that alters our personality, but the absence of love that prevents our more genuine aspects from coming to light. Instead of saying to the person who has fallen in love, "I don't recognize you anymore," we should say, "I never really knew you before this."

It is the person who has fallen in love who no longer recognizes himself. This is because hidden aspects of his personality have emerged, the existence of which he did not suspect. And this is why, since the beginning of recorded history, every culture has attempted to curb and tame so alarming a phenomenon, channeling its energy into rituals and institutions — engagement and matrimony, for example. When it is not molded into one of those forms, then love once again finds its original, elementary, and savage nature, often destructive because of the enormous quantity of energy liberated as the shadow finally emerges. Then, as never before, is the individual so unified, so strong, and in certain cases so devastating. It is a "state of grace" without the ethical connotations, and in it we are capable, as never before, of the most wonderful and most evil actions. We are able to discard like excess baggage anything standing in our way—career, duty, social restraints, and any previous bonds that might have been restricting us. It is the last of these—the previously contracted bonds—which most often become the point of contention. If one's emotional requirements and experiences, and subsequently their channeling by social pressures into ritual and institutional forms, were premature, it logically follows that finding oneself tied to a chosen partner will become tragic, for it is extremely difficult to remain forever true to a choice made when our emotional and sentimental life had only just begun. Very often, our mature encounters occur when we are already committed and bound by one of these prematurely contracted situations. However, it is fortunate for us that love is powerful enough to overcome social taboos, even if the price in suffering for doing so is high. Because we have been trained practically since birth to accept certain obligations, rejecting them inevitably causes an agonizing sense of guilt. But it is difficult to say objectively which is the more agonizing, the guilt or later regrets about not having done what we wanted to.

Once we have established that transference love is love, unqualified, it is only logical to ask whether these conflicts and agonizings do not also exist within the analytic setting. The answer is this is obviously yes, but with a few minor qualifications, which the myth of Eros and Psyche will help to make clear.

Psyche, overcome by curiosity, broke the pact she had made never to look directly into the face of her mysterious nocturnal lover. When she suddenly and irresistibly shed the light of her lantern on him, she discovered that, not only was he not a monster, he was Eros incarnate. But, alas, the very moment the divine beauty of her mysterious lover was revealed to her, she lost him. Eros vanished literally, and for Psyche the desperate search began for a love barely tasted and lost. What followed was a long ordeal of difficult rites which, in the end, were rewarded by Eros, who obtained from Zeus immortality for Psyche, thus making possible the union of their two destinies. As with all fables, this one can be interpreted on various levels. Platonists and neo-Platonists consider it the perfect example of certain mysterious practices; Christians consider it an allegory of the union of the soul with God in heavenly beatitude; we "moderns" can choose between an anthropological, psychological, or even psychoanalytic interpretation.

Clearly, the story of Eros and Psyche symbolizes the eternal and universal tale of true love conquering all. The first encounter reveals the fascination, but true love comes only much later, and not at the price of a simple transgression, but after a series of painful trials which mature the individual. Our analogy is even more to the point if we apply it to transference love, because it sheds light also on its proper conclusion: the patient/Psyche is united, at the end of a long and difficult journey fraught with peril, suffering, and obstacles, with the analyst/Eros, but on Olympus, and for eternity, that is, in a symbolic and, to quote Freud, "sublimated" form. The patient is united with love, rather than with the individual incarnating it, be he man or god.

This helps show exactly where the real difference lies between the love that blooms in the therapeutic setting and that which flowers outside it, and to determine the real elements — more concerned with therapy than the tranquility of the therapist — which indicate the appropriate reactions of the analyst to the patient's becoming enamored. If outside the analytic setting, we can hope that having made a premature love choice will not necessarily prevent growth, then in analysis, maintaining a distance is surely the only way to compel the patient to grow. The analyst/Eros must flee, in order to prevent the patient/Psyche from assuming paradoxically that he can both speed up his maturing process and actually avoid it. Only by stepping back can the analyst force the patient, step by step, on the road to maturity, in the same way that a parent, overcoming his desire to gather the child to him, moves backward when the small child learning to walk comes toward him with arms outstretched. This does not mean that he rejects love, but that he is using it for the good of the other.

We have said that, although the analyst has previously been analyzed, it is possible — even probable — that some remote and still hidden aspect of his personality will come to the fore in the dramatic atmosphere in which the transference neurosis is formed. In such cases, the patient has either been clever or lucky enough (the proverbial beginner's luck) to have zeroed in on a weak point, rendering the analyst as vulnerable as Siegfried. Then the analyst as well experiences firsthand the drama of Psyche, as he attempts to violate the pact by shedding light suddenly on his partner.

Such experiences are very painful because the analyst finds himself, as Jung would say, torn between duty (because his duties include following his own feelings) and doing his job (which is raising his patient's level of consciousness and encouraging psychological growth).

What behavior is appropriate in such a situation?

Freud's response was colored by one of the requirements of the historical epoch in which the budding profession of psychoanalysis was developing: the necessity of maintaining the emotional field without, however, giving satisfaction.

Unfortunately, as any psychotherapist knows from direct experience, this attitude is not the solution to the problem. It will serve at best to save the soul of the analyst; it will certainly not save the relationship or the patient. There is no single answer, no single strategy, because these situations are formed within unique relationships. They are the result of a combination of two individuals and thus require individual responses. In any case, whatever the solution, it is never painless. We are always between Scylla and Charybdis. And, speaking from personal experience, when things go badly, they do so because rising to the occasion is too difficult for the analyst. I believe this is due precisely to the fact that the analyst's choice of profession was dictated by that difficulty with object relationships to which we have referred more than once. As long as the analyst is protected by the charisma conferred upon him by his role, he is safe. The minute he steps out of his role, thus shedding that charisma, he is as exposed as anyone else, perhaps even more so, just because of that difficulty in relating, because of the unknown quantities in a relationship for which he was not particularly prepared.

Fourteen

The Transference of the Analyst

We have said that in the analytic relationship the patient is in a position of structural dependence.

We refer to the structure of analysis and not the personality of the analyst, because for some time we have known that this dependency occurs in any case, quite apart from any particular qualities of the therapist although these will have a decisive role during certain phases of the analysis. The fact is that, at the beginning of the analysis, it is difficult for the patient to bring into focus the real personality of the analyst, because the role of savior and the subsequent projections implicit in that role give the analyst an aura of unreality which blurs his image.

This idealization of the therapist is the result of at least two of the patient's unconscious desires. His overestimation of the analyst on the one hand reassures him that his hopes for salvation have some foundation, and on the other prepares the ground for the eventual venting of aggression. Having placed the therapist in a humanly untenable position, he has prepared the way for certain disappointment (Carotenuto 1980, p. 121).

Thus, the process of idealization is activated by two opposing motivations—the need to give oneself trustingly to another and the aggression felt toward that other—which end up reinforcing each other. We could further break down the more paradoxical of the two, aggression. This can be caused not only by the familiar ambivalence, duplicity, and deceitfulness of love in general, but also by factors particular to analysis such as the fact that the neurosis protects itself from being eliminated, attacking before being attacked. There is yet another, even more hidden, motivation: the preparation for mitigat-

ing or rendering less painful the separation when it becomes "physiologically" inevitable, checking possible disappointment. "I was basically afraid of not being able to do without you because I thought of
you as a god. Fortunately, you disappointed me." This is a healthy
motivation in that it is not the neurosis protecting itself, but the
future cure. But they combine and, as they are forces moving in the
same direction, strengthen each other.

These then are the roots of the patient's unrealistic expectations as
regards the therapy. Let us now consider some of the consequences of
this phenomenon. One of these is precisely the love transference. In a
relationship of dependence, the overestimation of the other means a
progressive alienation from oneself. The only instrument for communication feasible then is love transference, which removes in a single
stroke that cosmic distance.

Anna Freud, who dedicated a considerable part of her studies to
defense mechanisms, spoke of identification with the aggressor in
those cases where the reaction to threat is love, whether objective or
subjective. There is abundant documentation of this paradoxical
mechanism in history, journalism, fiction, and the cinema. We mentioned the Stockholm Syndrome. Another illustration is Italian film
director Liliana Cavani's *Night Porter*. The plot of this film translates
faithfully into dramatic terms Anna Freud's theory, according to
which love can be mobilized as a last resort in defending oneself
against a persecutor.

This can, and often does, occur also during analysis. The probabil-
ity of its occurring is even greater when the analyst's reserve (which is
also a defense, even though interpreted by the patient as hostility
because it frustrates) involuntarily pushes the patient in the direction
of seeking security in love. This is one of the reasons Sigmund Freud's
commandment unfortunately does not function.

It goes without saying that love is not always the only way out of a
situation when it appears to be the last resort. We know well enough
that the motivations and intentions for choosing that special form of
communication can also be quite unrelated to self-defense, for
example, a mutual exchange, a reciprocal gift benefitting both parties. If this is possible in "real" life, why shouldn't it also be possible
in the analytic setting?

It was, in fact, on similar theories that a current of psychotherapy
called existential psychotherapy was based. Binswanger, one of the

main exponents of this school, dealt — like Jung, and unlike Freud — with psychotics, and therapeutic relationships with this particular kind of patient led him to formulate original solutions and concepts. The conditions of a psychotic patient make it impossible for him to tolerate and constructively work out frustration, an inevitable element in the analysis of neurotics. Binswanger, instead of limiting himself simply to considering this contraindication, makes it the theme of his research and the basis of his therapeutic methods and their supporting theory. Briefly, if the patient's confidence in himself is so weakened that the least shock will destroy it, the most important thing to be done is to reinforce that nucleus, however slight, of self-esteem surviving.

Just as the pedagogic methods created by Montessori for subnormal children were subsequently applied in the education of normal children, so Binswanger's approach to the inner world of the psychotic spread, by a sort of osmosis, to psychotherapeutic procedure in general. In this light, the transference phenomenon is accepted and experienced as authentic and not considered an illusion, produced by the patient's disturbed state, or just another illness to be treated, one more of the endless demonstrations of the patient's inability to relate properly to reality.

And so, we have come a long way from the early definitions of transference. But, as we have said, it was essentially not harmful to the new psychoanalysis that attention was not immediately focused on the scandalous authenticity of the emotions existing within the therapeutic setting. We might even say with hindsight that it was a beneficial deception.

Let us attempt to make clear why countertransference is nothing more or less than the transference of the analyst, adding incidentally that barriers, even if only verbal, were not really necessary.

If it is true that the transference has the beneficial function of placing the patient in a state of grace, the same must be said of the analyst, that is, in the end he becomes a patient, too.

So far, so good. I believe that it is actually thus: the analyst will have gone through his own analysis, but that analysis will have been thorough and conclusive in the context of only one of the two functions assigned to didactic analysis. The future analyst places himself in analysis originally for two reasons: in order to understand himself and in order to understand the instruments necessary for reaching that understanding, the instruments with which the psychic world is probed. It is clear that the second can be achieved completely — nothing prevents the future analyst, at least in theory, from perfectly mastering the various techniques, albeit always limited by the present state of knowledge in the field. However, as regards the first, we must not have any illusions. Anything which has not been completely analyzed will necessarily remain. The psyche is like a bottomless well, and the analyst's own analysis is the first case of perpetual analysis he will encounter.

Incidentally, strictly speaking, we could say that all analyses are perpetual, although this term is normally used to define only those cases in which a decisive turning-point is never reached, in which the patient never contacts the reality of his own inner world which would have subsequently enabled him to go more deeply into his own unconscious without the analyst's help.

Stating that the analyst's own analysis is perpetual does not mean the matter ends there or that no further attempt should be made to progress. The acquired mastery of the cognitive instruments, one of the aims of didactic analysis, will permit the analyst to continue his own analysis, precisely through his work with his patients, which is in fact a further probing of his own psychic world. The basic instruments are acquired during the analytical training, but the principal means for probing the patient's inner nature will turn out to be the careful listening to and deciphering of the inner resonances the patient causes, from time to time, in the analyst.

The analyst must be on guard against overlooking, with that easy indulgence professionals often have toward themselves, the feelings of boredom or irritation, of expectation, fear, or desire that an individual patient provokes in him. He must instead concentrate on them, discover their deep origins in his own affective world. If an analysis seems endless, it means that something unknown within has blocked the analyst, that it is the analyst who is in a crisis, unable to resolve his new old unresolved problem, which was either never confronted or insufficiently analyzed during his didactic analysis. In other words, that famous resistance of the patient's has emerged in the analyst.

This is likeliest in a heterosexual analyst/patient relationship; in a rapport of this type the analyst is more directly confronted with his inner heterosexual counterpart — the anima for a male analyst. And it is this particular analytical situation which has traditionally been most often suspected of misdemeanor and continues to be to this day.

However, it should be borne in mind that, although it is true that in an analysis involving different sexes, Eros is present in a more concrete and palpable manner, the erotic element also presents a risk between a therapist and a patient of the same sex. This is because each one of us has within a sexual counterpart, and consequently, heterosexual elements are never absent. In Jungian terms, we could say that what appears to be a game *à deux* is actually always a *ménage à quatre* (Jung 1946, pp. 220–221). The true confrontation involves the inner heterosexual figures of which the analyst and the patient are the bearers. More often, however, in analyses where the sex of the patient and analyst is the same, transference phenomena are expressed on a different level than a specifically amorous one. One example would be competition with the figure of the parent of the same sex.

Going back to the heterosexual analytic couple, undoubtedly the snares and risks present and the level of mastery over emotions consequently required make this profession unsuitable for sorcerer's apprentices, who are too young, for emotional maturity is acquired through experience. However, no one will deny that chronological age alone is not an automatic and foolproof guarantee of maturity. A man of fifty who has never seriously been in love is still emotionally a child.

In any case, neither age nor experience can protect the analyst from those libidinal tempests which occur in his practice, for emotions — his own, as well as his patients' — are his chief instruments. The only difference between the two sets of emotions is the analyst's privileged position of having had long experience in testing his strength with various patients. That experience and variety of encounters, added to his specific training, give him the advantage of knowing thoroughly not only the rules of the game, but also the entire repertory of moves the patient might make. It is a little like a game in which only the patient lays his cards on the table; the analyst knows both his own cards and those of his adversary.

Nevertheless, despite those considerable advantages, the outcome is anything but assured; cards held in the hand can be as bad as those face up can be good. Such cases are fortunately rare — should the

121

therapist lose, it is the therapy which becomes bedlam and the patient's neurosis which wins out. One might ask how it is that the privileged position of the analyst does not always succeed in preventing defeat.

To choose the psychoanalyst's profession is to choose involvement in an endless succession of libidinal sacrifices, because it means living and working in love. And love always implies a promise—a promise, among other things, not to heed limitations or prohibitions. From time immemorial, and not only in novels or fairy tales, love has seemed destined above all to unite those separated by some insuperable barrier: princes and Cinderellas, ladies and gamekeepers, noblewomen and bandits all end up falling into each others' arms, no matter how dizzying the leap required. But the analyst who falls in love cannot permit himself the luxury of expecting the promise to be fulfilled. The patient has the right to expect the impossible, but the therapist is bound to contain (both in the Latin sense of "comprising within himself" and in the sense of "restraining") the emotions of the patient, without either rejecting or extinguishing them. He must welcome them and give them form, utilizing them in the best possible way, as the waters of a dam are used, when contained, to produce energy.

It is just this necessity of collecting the flood of emotion without being submerged by it, to give it form, that renders the analyst's self-imposed renunciation so difficult. No wall exists between himself and the patient, only a sword like the one uniting and separating Tristan and Isolde sleeping in the same bed. And with the passing of time, accumulating experience, and maturing of the analyst, the way of renunciation, far from becoming easier, becomes even more difficult. A wall can be reinforced, but the analyst's growth, if anything, increases his emotional capacity, and time, as we know, intensifies unsatisfied desire. It is not at all inconceivable that one day the analyst may come up with a rational pretext for permitting himself a bit of satisfaction, that is, transgression. He might actually end up theorizing, for example, that it is just the experience of confronting a bit of reciprocal satisfaction which is needed for his emotional growth; or that the very fact that the patient has hit upon some unresolved deeper problem requires it, so that the psychoanalyst can confront radically that new and crucial situation, regardless of the consequences; or that this particular patient and this particular case cannot be dealt with in any other way. Or, he might espouse the promising theory that breaking the rule is as significant and illuminating as the rule itself, perhaps even more so, as long as it is done consciously and for the purpose of acquiring knowledge, and so on, into the night. We know well enough how simple it is to find a plausible rationalization for satisfying a pressing emotional need, one which will render that need presentable and justify it in our own eyes. Since rationalizations have been found for satisfying the obscure need to defend ourselves from emotions, why shouldn't they also be found to do the opposite?

In fact, whether or not he is aware of it, the patient aims at driving the analyst out of his ivory tower, his fortress. And the patient is not mistaken there. The analyst's defenses must be destroyed, and the analyst must learn to stop protecting himself, not only from the emotions of the patient — that is, the transference — but also from his own — the countertransference. But it is one thing not to prohibit one's own feelings in order to experience intimately their sense and force, to master them and use them, and quite another to unconditionally accept all demands and thus become controlled by them.

Fifteen

Caught in the Trap

Homo sapiens did not invent seduction. In an infinite variety of
species not only could the ritual behavior preceding mating be
defined as seductive, but as ethologists inform us, even the tender,
awkward comportment of the young of many species is nothing more
than an unconscious seductive mechanism which transforms their
relative weakness into a practically infallible means of defense against
larger members of their species and sometimes others, including
humans. Mature domestic animals, in their relationship to man,
apply not only the seductive behavior originally devised by Mother
Nature for purposes of sexual selection, but also that behavior usually
reserved to the young of the species for its own protection.

Undoubtedly, humans have developed and refined this natural
defense to the point of making it an art, albeit a minor one. We have
already said that seduction is the most common strategy for dealing
with the difficult problems inherent in relationships. Thus, it is
inevitable that in the analytic setting, which is model and "mansion"
of the two-person relationship, the legal tender should be seduction.

Although the advent of language provided the prospective seducer
with an additional weapon, the most effective means of seduction
obviously is not verbal, even though often enough words act as its
vehicle, carrying it, hidden, like a stowaway, to its destination. True
seduction consists of imperceptible signals and works in silence.

We have already said that the analyst also seduces—whether he
intends to or not, whether he admits to it or not—for technical
reasons and by vocation. It is not usually necessary for him to be
particularly insightful to obtain his desired result, which is the transference, since from the outset he can count on the automatic effect of

his position (the charisma we referred to above). However, when it is the patient who seduces, the game becomes far more subtle, because the patient knows, or supposes, that he has before him an exceptionally shrewd adversary, an expert in the game at hand, a veteran in the field. Thus, there is the danger that those imperceptible signals may remain unnoticed until that moment when the analyst can do little more than take note simultaneously of the seductive action and the fact that it has succeeded. Of the two, the analyst is the better equipped to protect himself from seduction. He is also the one who, precisely by virtue of his knowledge of the rules of the game and the repertory of possible moves, least expects to be checkmated.

It is at this point that the analyst realizes suddenly that something has changed in his relationship with the patient. That "something" is certainly not a mere detail, since it is capable of altering his inner reality, of creating a new gestalt in his psychological world. The patient (the female patient) has become indispensable, not only a habit, but also an addiction.

The appearance of the patient in the analyst's dreams can be a warning signal that this is happening. Our psychological order normally permits us to "metabolize" our experiences, even the most significant, in other words, to extract their sense and worth, thus enriching our psychic patrimony. If in our dreams we relive a daytime experience with its real connotations, it means the experience has not been metabolized, but swallowed whole, existing inside us like the prophet Jonah in the belly of the whale. It means that the experience provoked an excessively controlling response, which prevented it from being worked out consciously and deposited it intact into our unconscious. There it is proposed to us again, compelling us to relive it in a sort of repetition compulsion on the oneiric level, always, however, with the intention of controlling its pressing emotional charge. In other words, something has not functioned as it should at the level of the defense of the ego; the analyst who dreams of his patient would do well to ask himself what it means.

After about six months of therapy with a patient, an analyst dreams that he is walking down a certain mountain path. He is surprised by the situation, and when he comes to a particularly steep stretch, he asks the patient to pass him a lamp, which she has brought along. The patient complies with his request and, besides the lamp, offers him her hand. With that lamp and holding the patient's hand, the analyst and the patient together begin the descent.

It is not difficult to discern in this dream an alarming reversal of roles in the analytic couple. It is the analyst who asks the patient for a lamp to light his way through the darkness during his descent into the underworld, and it is the patient who offers him not only her lamp but a helping and reassuring hand as well. Dante and Virgil have exchanged parts: Virgil, the master, implores Dante to act as his guide and it is he who must utter the sad, "Have mercy on me." Whoever has had the good fortune to read Jung's letters to Sabina Spielrein, the publication of which has been prohibited by her heirs, cannot fail to remember one of the most distressing of them, in which, not by chance, the most adamant refusal comes from the one still having the right of veto.

That letter demonstrates with dramatic eloquence the reversal of roles. The "witch bewitched" admits to weakness, unhappiness, insecurity. He states that his destiny is in the hands of his by-now ex-patient, whose judgment and possibly even revenge he fears. He is afraid of being ridiculed if he dares confide in her. He is besieged by memories of early infancy and thoughts of death. Above all, he implores a bit of tenderness for what he once gave to her when she was just a patient.

At this point, one might well ask why this situation—rare, but not impossible nor entirely unexpected in the private and professional life of an analyst—should cause him so much anxiety, inspire so many fears. Let us say first off that those fears were not unfounded. The analyst fears because he is only too well aware of the dynamics that characterize the analytic relationship and that induce the inherently ambivalent transference. The idealization of the analyst, the overestimation of the love object, results in the patient accepting a disparaging self-image. Whosoever makes a god of another inevitably makes of himself a wretch. It is inevitable that so frustrating a concept of oneself will create—as a counterpoint to love—the secret need and desire to destroy the living proof of that state of insignificance.

This ambivalence, the glaring presence of the aggression component in the analytic relationship, must, when the patient realizes that he has the upper hand over the other who so recently dominated and annihilated him, push him to take advantage of the reversal, giving vent finally to the aggression. We know that there is no more devastating form of aggression than the one produced within the love relationship. Even the aggression involved in the struggle for power is child's play compared to the violence that can be unleashed when the relationship between the aggressor and his victim is a sentimental one.

Thus, we might say that the analyst who dreamt that his patient offered him her lamp and led him by the hand down a steep path was most certainly warned by that oneiric message of what was happening, or better still, of what had already happened in the underground of his psychic life, and what could happen, or rather was to happen, in the analytic relationship. In his fantasy life, an anima figure had been evoked capable of challenging all the rules of the game. What happens in the analytic setting is what happened to our colleague; that is, the patient realized that the relationship had changed, felt that the analyst needed her, and unconsciously set about taking her revenge for all the wounds inflicted to her self-esteem up to that time. As she no longer feared losing him, she could give free rein to all the aggression stored up during the positive transference.

In another troubling case, this time involving a female analyst and a male patient, the patient was passed on from one analyst to another. Gifts of this kind are usually Trojan horses, and in fact the patient in question was a difficult one. He was an alcoholic, and alcoholism, like all neuroses of an oral character, is difficult to treat because its origins go back to a very early phase of development. The more remote the causes of a disorder, the less hope there is of resolving it. The original therapist, not having succeeded in getting to the root of the problem, passed it on to his colleague.

Why a Trojan horse? Because, if giving up on a patient with whom one has not succeeded can be interpreted as a simple, objective, and realistic admission of failure, then passing on that patient to a colleague can be interpreted as a more or less premeditated act of aggression. The donor knew from direct experience that he was presenting his colleague with a desperate case.

The original analyst and the subsequent analyst were, besides being colleagues, also living together. This does not, however, make the concept less conceivable. In fact it is more plausible, since within a couple practicing the same profession there is inevitably a certain degree of rivalry, which although hidden is nonetheless there, like underground streams that only at certain points emerge into the light of day.

Thus, our analyst accepted the new patient as though accepting a challenge from her companion, as though to prove to him as well as to herself that she could succeed where he had failed. She applied herself to that hopeless task with such fervor that she ended up falling desperately in love with her patient.

If it is true that love knows no bounds, then it is not surprising that, when all else has failed to form a relationship, it should be the last card played. We have seen how the patient resorts to this solution when he feels hemmed in. Now we must accept the idea of the therapist doing the same.

I should like to point out here that the colleague in question is an able and experienced professional. Yet neither ability nor experience prevented her from choosing and following to the very end a road not only fraught with danger and full of obstacles, but, more seriously, at cross purposes to her original intention, which was to cure her patient. She subsequently left her companion and went to live with her alcoholic patient. Obviously, in her fury to heal, she believed that so total an act of dedication would in the end be rewarded, and that her own psychic well-being could not fail to influence her patient-lover. Of course, things did not turn out quite that way. What did happen was the exact opposite: the progressive breakdown of the analyst. She was forced literally to empty herself day after day, although the emotional nourishment she provided her patient had no effect whatsoever, because not only is an oral patient emotionally a child, he is absolutely incapable of assimilating, of "metabolizing," such nourishment.

Fortunately, certain descents into the underworld are not irreversible. Sometimes events intercede which it would be too cynical to call miraculous, but which all the same change the course of events when the outcome had seemed irremediably decided. So destructive a patient may succeed in destroying himself before he has destroyed the other, or else go so far afield that the other is unable to keep up. Without going into further detail, I will say that the analyst in question did manage to emerge from that experience and, more importantly, succeeded in metabolizing it. The experience in the end was not something from her personal life to be forgotten or rejected as foreign, "so full of sleep was she at the time." Even if the sleep of reason generates monsters, having measured one's strength against those monsters is an obligatory step, an unavoidable trial on the way to growth.

I have told this story because it is a revealing example of how a patient's attempt to seduce can prevail if it succeeds in playing unconsciously on some unresolved problem of the analyst's. In this case, the problem was probably related to the analyst's need to measure herself against a man who seemed less fearsome—an oral type, a man who was still a child. It is also an example in a more general sense of how passage from an analytic relationship to a love relationship plays upon the patient's relative weakness and the secret need of the analyst to have the upper hand in emotional relationships (Lester 1985; Schwartz-Salant 1984; Taylor 1982; Ulanov 1979; Carotenuto 1986).

When we spoke of the ways in which the therapist rationalizes his need to transgress, we omitted those extreme, and thus statistically irrelevant, cases in which such rationalization coincides with the abnormal logic of neurosis. In these cases, the therapist *literally* needs to go into therapy. In fact, Sydney Smith (1984), of the California School of Professional Psychology in San Diego, tells us that he had in treatment for some months one such "abusing therapist." I do not think it necessary to point out here that this expression does not refer to unqualified analysts, but rather to those who take advantage of the patient. Obviously, the didactic analyses of such analysts have left not merely a few blanks, but such abysses that actually accusing them of improper or incompetent practice might not be entirely out of line.

But let us consider the explanation offered by Smith of the behavior of one of these abusing therapists. The analyst in question is just over forty years of age and divorced. He identifies with the patient's suffering and decides to relieve that suffering by gratifying her in some way—a kindly attitude, some small gift. Subsequently, the analyst becomes convinced that the patient owes him a debt of gratitude, which must be "honored." When the patient appears unwilling to acknowledge this obligation, the analyst feels a growing sense of anger toward her, which soon enough is expressed by a coldly aggressive attitude. The analyst becomes caustic and venomous to the extent that the patient is finally convinced the only way to placate the analyst's anger is to give herself to him. Here Smith concludes with the shrewd observation that in the heterosexual analytic couple, the one harboring unrealistic expectations of Eros is usually the patient, not the analyst.

In such cases it is not the credibility of our work which should come under fire, any more than progress made in the field of surgery is called into question when an individual surgeon errs. What is relevant to our topic is only what is inevitable in the patient/analyst relationship, an emotional bond based on affection which necessarily and normally assumes certain characteristics. Indeed, these characteristics will be heightened, as ours is an experimental situation which magnifies and focuses like a lens, making possible a clearer interpretation.

One of those characteristics—as old as man himself and dating back to the dawn of history when an indiscriminate Eros was set aside for a directed one—is the need to continue on in time, beyond the simple satisfaction of erotic desire.

For this reason, it is more precise to refer to a "relationship" than to a "rapport," which could cease after a single encounter. Continuing on in time means growing together and not simply in each other's presence. It means a mutual nourishing. The destinies of the two are united, become one. And yet, when it comes to admitting this characteristic, even in the model of the emotional relationship which analysis is, the instinct rises up in many of us to rebel, often armed with solid theoretical objections.

It is worth citing at least two such objections, the most frequent. The first is that it is the experimental nature itself of the analytic relationship that compromises in some way its authenticity, making it different from a "normal" relationship. This of course justifies denying it all the connotations characterizing a relationship formed spontaneously. The second objection, astonishing in its simplicity, points out the multiplicity of the analyst's partners (since it is unlikely that the patient will have more than one analyst) in order to distinguish clearly the therapist's involvement from that of each of his patients.

To the first objection, which makes the experimental nature of the analytic relationship a sort of original sin, the shadow of which spreads over the entire process, ultimately devaluing it (cultivated pearls being so much less prized than those formed naturally), we could offer some serious counter-objections. We could point out for example that in a situation created (or recreated) in a laboratory for ease of observation or verification, the dynamics brought into play—whatever the methods used to create them—are exactly the same as those produced spontaneously in analogous circumstances outside the laboratory. Otherwise the experiment would be pointless. But then, how many "normal" relationships (that is, those outside the analytic setting) can we say with any certainty are formed spontaneously? What else is seduction, the first move in any love game, if not the art of provocation, sowing the seeds, and forcing love, instead of waiting for it to flower spontaneously? And isn't the meaning of "love that nothing beloved pardons" perhaps that the simple act of loving is in its own way extorting love? It is useless to try to deceive ourselves. When a sentiment is formed, no matter how, it exists overwhelmingly and vitally, and there is no point in asking for certificates of legitimacy.

As to the second objection, regarding the multiplicity of the analyst's partners and distinguishing between the transference of the analyst and that of each of his patients, it might become valid the day it is proved that each human being has limited and anything-but-inexhaustible emotional reserves, upon which he must draw with moderation if he is to avoid being left high and dry. (This is vaguely reminiscent of the Sicilian theory of a limited number of ejaculations allotted each male to last him his entire career as a lover.) Or when it is confirmed that human nature is profoundly and irremediably monogamous. Until such a time, it would be well to give a bit of credit to those sailors who claim that, although they have a girl in every port, in every port that girl is the only girl in the world. For now, we are justified in thinking that any analyst who has developed his inner resources, increasing the range of his own capacity to relate, is in a position to form various relationships, each of which is authentic and unique.

Thus, I do not consider it rash to have asserted that roles within the analytic relationship are absolutely reciprocal, or that the destinies of the two (patient and analyst) become one. Any analyst can report that a great many of the psychological turning points and stages of inner development in his life were stimulated by the impact of various patients.

The patient's presence continually activates contents in the unconscious of the analyst, who must be receptive to the problems and suffering of the patient in order to succeed in literally making that content his own, that is, recognizing within himself its presence, which until then had been latent and vague but is now alive and clearly perceived. In other words, the patient, by bringing his conflicts into the analytic relationship, causes the analyst to acquire a clear awareness of some personal problem of his own which has either not emerged before, or at least was not dealt with properly during didactic analysis. Thus, the patient unconsciously offers his analyst the same opportunity for transformation which, as a rule and "institutionally," the analyst offers him.

Although it is justifiable that the patient be unconscious of what is happening, the analyst absolutely cannot permit himself a similar luxury. The condition *sine qua non* allowing him to profit by that unexpected opportunity the patient offers him is a lucid, implacable, and unrelenting process of becoming aware of the new conflict that has emerged. Because, although awareness of a problem does not automatically guarantee its solution, without awareness there can be no transformation of any sort. Thus the analyst's most important task is to take note of the countertransference, gradually, as it becomes activated by the patient's presence.

This means that we must add another rule, just as important, to the ethical demand that the analyst listen attentively to the patient: that he listen attentively to himself, lending an ear to the resonance which the patient's words provoke inside him. If that resonance is lacking, there are two possible explanations: either the patient's problems absolutely do not touch the analyst because they are truly alien to him, or else he is protecting himself.

The first of these explanations obviously does not interest us here, since where there is no true interest, there can certainly be no countertransference. I would not wish on any patient or, for that matter, on any analyst, a relationship that sooner or later must turn out to be frustrating for both. However, if there is a countertransference, and the detachment of the analyst reveals that he is simply protecting himself, then it must be said that his attitude is doubly false. He is being false both to himself, as he is protecting and preserving his own personal status quo instead of taking advantage of the chance to grow and progress along the road to individuation, and to his patient, because by turning a deaf ear to his countertransference, to his inner resonances, he deliberately renounces utilizing emotional information the interpretation of which could shed precious light on the patient's problems.

By ignoring his own reactions and removing from the sphere of observation an essential component, the analyst falsifies the significance of what occurs within the setting. And, what is more, by renouncing its interpretation, he is guilty of the same offense for what he has more or less explicitly reproached the patient—that of unloading onto others or external reality the entire responsibility for vicissitudes, frustrations, and failure. For example, if the analyst reacts to a patient complaining of his coldness by returning the whole problem of the patient's neurosis, the idea of the relationship being contaminated by unreasonable demands and unrealistic expectations as exclusively the patient's, isn't the analyst withdrawing and placing the responsibility on the patient for all his own interior agitation, discomfort, conflict, apprehension, his secret hopes or fears, in the same way the anchorite found it necessary to conceive of the devil as something outside himself?

This is an ethical problem, and here I shall not speak of rules. It is not correct, honest, or moral for the analyst to fail to expect of himself what he expects of his patient, that is, not to be satisfied with soothing rationalizations in order to maintain an uncertain—and improbable—inner peace.

When I am accused of coldness by a patient and feel that accusation charged with aggressivity, I will make no progress in the therapy if I adopt the usual *fin de non-recevoir*, returning that aggressivity to the sender, indicating him as the legitimate owner of the phantasms of parental figures of himself. The moment will come when I must accept the fact that I am personally involved and acknowledge the involvement. By dodging the blows, I am actually delivering a powerful blow to the patient, placing him in a condition of crisis because I am his proof of reality. I have come into play without wishing to. But the Jungian theory of therapy requires that I compromise myself, that I run risks, in those crucial moments of the relationship. It requires that I become part of the patient's affairs, that I open myself to him, just as he opens himself to me, to the extent of confiding in him, even telling him *my* dreams, if that would be of help in his redemption (Carotenuto 1970a, 1970b).

Sixteen

The Separation

The moment must come when the analytic relationship ends with the breaking up of the couple. It is an inevitable conclusion if the analyst is to achieve what he set out to do. It is one of the few examples where separation in an emotional relationship means success and not failure.

The analyst is aware of this eventuality from the beginning of the relationship. The patient becomes progressively aware of it as the analysis proceeds. In fact, it is sometimes the dreams of the patient himself which transmit to the analyst the unmistakable message that the moment has come.

Awareness does not, however, alter the fact that it is a painful loss for both the patient and the analyst—even if the latter is not only professionally prepared, but actually a veteran in such experiences, having gone through it as many times as he has treated patients. Prepared, experienced, but not immunized—for ours is a profession in which immunity is detrimental; in order to work well, we need our sensitivity preserved intact (Carotenuto 1979).

Experiencing the separation without pain would mean suddenly denying all significance to the relationship. Apropos of this, Freud commented—firmly and to the point—that we must experience the loss, feel nostalgia, because only in this way do we bestow dignity upon the relationship. In any event, the end of a love—as both transference and countertransference are—even if agreed to by common consent, even if mutually considered to be right and useful, cannot fail to cause grief and melancholy. The process is somewhat like the negative impression left in the center of our field of vision, in the exact same shape but filled with darkness, of the light into which we looked for a while.

Our discourse becomes more subtle when we consider how we can and must experience this inevitable pain. To experience something, anything, actively is so profoundly different from experiencing it passively; it means actually having participated, having done our part, on our own. When it is a question of an emotional experience such as grief, it also means working out the inner lost love, transforming the loss into energy.

Not only is the analyst specifically experienced in working out the separation, paradoxically, from the very beginning of the analysis, he has prepared the way for the relationship's eventual end. He knows that the dependence of the patient, besides being inevitable and desirable, is an element to work with in the therapy, but also that the patient's emancipation is the desired end result.

This means that, for the patient, the ability to work out the separation will coincide with the necessity to act upon it; it is, in other words, the maturing process for which the therapy was initially undertaken, the liberation of the patient's capacities, including creativity, the inhibition of which is the origin of all psychic discomfort and suffering.

To illustrate the type of dependence the patient experiences in analysis, we have referred most frequently to that relationship model called uroboros, in which the mother "contains" the infant until it has developed — in a sort of second birth — the ego–Self axis which gives the individual the strength to live in the world with a minimum of inner security, the ability to defend himself without having to search continually outside himself for protection.

In this dyadic relationship, which we could define as pre-oedipal, there is for the moment no room for a third party. And yet, the eventual entrance of a third party is inevitably prepared by that growth, or second birth, which is occurring in the warm uroboric womb. In the child's history, the third party comes onto the scene during the oedipal phase, along with the alarming discovery that the true setting of the affective life is not the uroboric paradise. In the analytic relationship, as in love relationships in general, this discovery has long before been made and established in our memory; thus, the phantasm of the third party come to drive us out of Eden easily gains ground.

If the figure of the third party does not appear, then it is imagined, since at this point it is functional in the adult love structure. The need for this figure is actually felt as concrete proof of reality, a guarantee of the authenticity of the bond.

In fact, an emotional relationship would not be conceivable without the third party, real or imagined; it paradoxically renders the couple situation dynamic, provoking the opportunity for improving communication and strengthening the relationship.

Within the analytic setting, after the initial period, the patient begins to fantasize about the people surrounding the analyst. Even if he has not had the opportunity of either meeting or knowing them, he is aware of the existence of other patients, who like himself are part of the relational world of his analytic partner. The content of such fantasies typically involve anxieties such as: "Will that be a special relationship?" "Will he care more about that one than he does about me?" These doubts, far from damaging or discouraging the transference, reinforce it in the same way a similar situation would reinforce an ordinary love relationship. Many couples begin to communicate once again after a third party appears, challenging the soundness of their bond.

In the complex emotional game of analysis, the analyst can find himself also in the role of third party to the couple made up of the patient and his external partner (married or otherwise). However, in this particular case it is improbable that the appearance of a third party will favor a rekindling of the flame or a strengthening of the bond, because the situation becomes complicated when the patient's growth comes into play, a development not accompanied by an analogous growth of his external partner.

This exception noted, let us return to those cases in which the appearance of the third party — real or imagined — energizes the relationship. We know, for example, how frequently in sentimental outpourings, one of the two partners fantasizes about the other's unfaithfulness. This is a fairly elementary mechanism, one in which interest and desire become stronger if there is, or it is imagined that there is, someone competing for the beloved object. But the most important aspect of this phenomenon, and not by chance bound up with our earliest experiences, is that the third party represents social reality, the exterior.

In classical Greek, the language that taught not only to name objects but also to conjugate them, to relate them, to divide them into singular and plural, there is a double singular: the true plurality begins with three. In fact, despite what popular songs and books of instruction in the writing of love letters tell us, "you and I" can never be the world. A couple relationship, complete and exclusive, and potentially symbiotic, runs the risk of alienating. By dint of sharing and identifying, the two partners risk losing their own identities. Thus, the Oedipus complex involves far more than incestuous desire, taking on vast significance. It can be interpreted as the individual opening up to the world.

In the infantile stage the third party is the father, who tears the child from the maternal uroboros; in the analytic situation, the emergence in the patient's psychic world of the fantasm of the third party has a similar function. Its purpose is to damage the uroboric shell of the relationship as it has been experienced up to that time by the patient, isolated within the "womb" of the analyst-mother.

Fear of the analytic relationship can be so strong that the third party appears immediately, as if to protect against a relationship vaguely intuited as being too involved and, more important, temporary. Usually, however, the third party enters the scene at the proper moment, that is, when the analyst also (if he knows his job and has subtly worked to prepare a space for it in the patient's psychic world) feels the necessity and the timeliness of the intrusion disturbing the too-calm waters of the setting and upsetting a harmony inappropriate because it does not reflect outside reality. The emancipation, or weaning, of the patient begins at this point.

We could also define the entrance of a third party into the affective world of the patient in analysis as a new sort of transference, beneficial in view of that initiation into reality which is, together with individuation, the objective toward which the analyst works. As to the actual transference, although it may be true that its resolution is the condition *sine qua non* for the breaking up of the analytic couple, I have the impression that this problem has been dramatically exaggerated. It is more to the point to ask what of that complex emotional structure we call transference can and should be eliminated. The most sensible response to this is: those exalted projections which represent its most infantile and unrealistic component (Kohut 1971).

The withdrawal of these projections will render the image of the analyst more plausible, but not necessarily less lovable. The mystery and fascination of a human being are often no less than those of a divine being, so much so that God felt the need to put to test a man by the name of Job.

On the other hand, if it is true—as so many anthropologists claim, literally reversing the biblical texts—that man created God in his own image and likeness, then how are we to distinguish what is divine in man and human in God?

We can say this much: after the separation, the patient will feel more nostalgia for the human-analyst than for the quality of divinity which he had attributed to him in his novitiate's fervor. However, I personally prefer that even this transfiguring and altering aspect, no longer legal tender in the patient's psychic world, never be entirely destroyed. It is my experience that in those ex-patients of mine whom I occasionally see, that anachronistic and obsolete image has been somehow preserved in their inner pantheon. Within all of us the dethroned figures of the first gods of our infancy remain.

Conclusions

The theme of this book has been the difficult progress of transference in its struggle to be recognized in psychotherapeutic theory, from the very dawn of dynamic psychology, when it was not even mentioned because it existed without an explanation, through the period when its existence was unceremoniously denied, on up to the point where it was admitted, at first as a sporadic and unfortunate occurrence, then as a beneficial *qui pro quo*, and finally to when the designation of "sporadic and unfortunate accident" was shifted to the transference of the analyst — or the countertransference.

The question could be put as to why this particular problem was chosen over other, perhaps even more important, ones — for instance, aspects of transference in psychotherapeutic situations differing from the classic heterosexual analyst/patient couple, more precisely, a male analyst and a female patient. (Ellenberger maintains that all the "important" cases in the history of transference concern this couple.)

The answer is that, on the long road toward the total legitimization of transference and its adoption as a therapeutic instrument, we analysts still have one last lap to run, and that is the legitimization and utilization of *our* transference, which not by chance was, and continues to be, defined as countertransference. This is a term which, in the appetizing theory of Lakoff and Johnson on the criptometaphor of word choice, might prompt us to read between the lines that one concept of this phenomenon is so loaded with apprehension and hostility as to be expressed instinctively in the language of military strategists (Lakoff and Johnson 1980, p. 33).

We have still to accept not only the inevitability, but also the functional capacity, of our love for the patient, even if this involves assuming a considerable degree of risk and the even more considerable task of maintaining equilibrium and control. We have cited the story of Eros and Psyche and their metaphorical union on Olympus, and we have mentioned Tristan's sword, which separates not the analyst from his patient, but love from its real, carnal consummation. But the issue of the extraordinary restraint that must be exercised by the analyst to maintain equilibrium and control prompts us to add to Courtly Love and the Idealized Patient yet another metaphor—the indefinite postponement of conclusion or culmination practiced and preached by oriental and Middle Eastern, as well as Western cultures, although in various ways and sometimes toward opposite ends. It is the basis of the Chinese *Tao*, certain tantric techniques, the Moslem *Imsak* and the Western *Karezza* and *coitus Reservatus*. It goes without saying that the most poetic description of this concept is given by the Chinese:

> Sex of peace and not of violence, an enduring smile rather than a burst of laughter, a long, reciprocal nourishing of the Yin and the Yang, male force and female force, instead of instant fusion which at very high temperatures would burn the two elements in a single bonfire. (Chang 1977)

As to those cases involving analytic couples other than the one described here as classic, it should be obvious that a theme so vast and complex requires a separate treatment. However, I might just say that it appears vast and more complex in proportion to the extent that the sexual roles are taken literally. Undeniably, judging from a rigorous and schematic standpoint, there existed at the beginning a substantial contradiction between certain psychoanalytical theories and the therapeutic practices of their creators. In an age and social ambience when the physician's patient was practically always a woman, Freud conceived and refined his Oedipus complex to the measure of man. And that was probably not so much due to some antiquated male chauvinism as to the fact that he was after all his own best patient— the only one he could investigate from within. But when a female child instead of a male child is placed in the center of an oedipal situation, the model cannot be applied as it stands, and neither can it be reversed, since for every individual there is first the mother and not the parent of the opposite sex.

However, for a Jungian the problem and its possible reverberations in the analytic setting are, or should be, less alarming; the presence in each individual of both the male and female figures, the animus and the anima, permits, even highlights, that game of opposites which in the analytic setting means the beginning of an authentic transference (although Jung maintained that in the heterosexual analytic couple, the interplay is richer and clearer).

A final observation on this concept of the two transferences (the patient's and the analyst's): although these transferences come to light in a kind of experimental laboratory (the setting), this does not mean that the roots and their nourishing ground derive any less from the patient's personal history or from the analyst's. The patient's expectations release the love-at-first-sight mechanism in the analyst, but the love relationship that develops is nourished, as it would be in any love situation, by the psychic world of both partners, thus including the path each of them has followed up to the time of their encounter.

There is yet another reason for maintaining that the treatment of the patient begins long before the first appointment is made, even before the time of the analyst's training: the remote events occurring in the past of the analyst which favored and motivated his choice of profession. The history of a treatment begins before the patient comes onto the scene, somewhat the way Laurence Sterne's novel, *The Life and Opinions of Tristam Shandy, Gentleman*, begins before the main character is born. Who can say whether perhaps one day, in the not-too-distant future, the expounding of a noteworthy case might begin as follows: "In my earliest childhood, according to what I have been told. . . ."

References

Balint, M. 1968. *Primary Love and Psycho-Analytic Technique*. London: The Hogarth Press.

Balint, M., and Balint, E. 1953. *The Basic Fault*. London: Tavistock Publications.

Baudrillard, J. 1979. *Della seduzione*. Bologna: Cappelli.

Belfiore, G. 1928. *Magnetismo e ipnotismo [Magnetism and Hypnotism]*. Milan: Hoepli.

Berman, L. 1949. Countertransference and attitudes of the analyst in the therapeutic process. *Psychiatry* 12:159–166.

Bettelheim, B. 1960. *The Informed Heart*. Glencoe: The Free Press.

Boille, E. 1985. Mesmer e gli albori della psicoanalisi. Unpublished manuscript. Rome: Corso de laurea in psicologia.

Bontempelli, M. 1928. *Opere scelte*. Milan: Mondadori, 1978.

Brenner, C. 1976. *Psychoanalytic Techniques and Psychic Conflict*. New York: International Universities Press.

Buber, M. 1954. *Il principio dialogico*. Milan: Edizioni di Comunità, 1959.

Carotenuto, A. 1970a. Observazioni su alcuni aspetti del transfert e controtransfert. *Rivista di Psicologia Analitica* 1:125–156.

_____. 1970b. A proposito della tecnica junghiana. *Rivista di Psicologia Analitica* 1:291–304.

_____. 1972. Psicopatologia dell'analista. *Rivista di Psicologia Analitica* 3:418–440.

_____. 1979. *La scala che scende nell'acqua*. Torino: Boringhieri.

_____. 1980. *Diario di una segreta simmetria. Sabina Spielrein tra Jung e Freud*. Rome: Astrolabio. English translation, *Diary of a Secret Symmetry*. New York: Pantheon Books, 1982.

_____. 1983. Nevrosi, processo creativo e potere sull'altro. *Rivista di Psicologia Analitica* 27:62–75.

_____. 1986. L'immagine nucleare. Bulletin for the Second Congress of the Italian Association for the Study of Analytical Psychology, Assisi.

Céline. L. F. 1952. *Il dottor Semmelweis*. Milan: Adelphi, 1975.

Chang, J. 1977. *The Tao of Love and Sex*. London: Wild Wood House, Ltd.

Chertok, L. 1968. The discovery of the transference. *International Journal of Psycho-Analysis* 49:560–577.

_____. 1979. *L'ipnosi tra psicoanalisi e biologia*. Milan: Celuc, 1981.

Chertok, L., and De Saussure, R. 1973. *Freud prima di Freud: Nacsita della psicoanalisi [Freud Before Freud]*. Bari: Laterza, 1975.

Cremerius, J. 1984. La regola psicoanalitica dell'astinenza. Dall'uso secondo la regola a quello operativo. *Psicoterapia e scienze Unane* 19:3–36.

_____. 1985. *Il mestiere dell'analista*. Torino: Boringhieri.

De Broglie, L. 1956. Nuove prospettive in microfisica. Milan: Fabbri, 1969.

Dehing, J. 1981. Il transfert come droga. *Rivista di Psicologia Analitica* 23:35–52.

De Saussure, R. 1963. Transference and animal magnetism. *Psychoanalytic Quarterly* 12:194–201.

De Villers, C. 1787. *Le magnétiseur amoureux*. Paris: Vrin, 1978.

Dinnerstein, A. 1976. *The Mermaid and the Minotaur*. New York: Harper and Row.

Edinger, E. F. 1960. The ego-Self paradox. *Journal of Analytical Psychology* 5:3–18.

Ehrenwald, J. 1966. *Psychotherapy: Myth and Method. An Integrative Approach*. New York: Grune and Stratton.

_____. 1976. *The History of Psychotherapy: From Healing Magic to Encounter*. New York: Jason Aronson, Inc.

Eissler, K. R. 1953. The effect of the structure of the ego on psychoanalytic technique. *Journal of the American Psychoanalytic Association* 1:104–143.

_____. 1982. *Psychologische Aspekte des Briefwechsels zwischen Freud and Jung*. Stuttgart: Frommann-Holzberg.

Ellenberger, H. F. 1970. *The Discovery of the Unconscious*. London: The Penguin Press.

Farrell, B. A. 1981. *The Standing of Psycho-Analysis*. Oxford: Oxford University Press.

Fenichel, O. 1941. *Problemi di tecnica psicoanalitica.* Torino: Boringhieri, 1974. English translation, *Problems of Psychoanalytic Technique*, David Brunswick, trans. New York: Psychoanalytic Quarterly, 1941.

Ferenczi, S. 1931. Child analysis in the analysis of adults. In *Problems and Methods of Psycho-Analysis: Selected Papers*, vol. 3. New York: Basic Books.

Feyerabend, P. K. 1971. *I problemi dell'empirismo*. Milan: Lampugnani Nigri Editore.

_____. 1978. *Il realismo scientifico e l'autorità della scienza*. Milan: Il Saggiatore, 1983.

Fliess, R. 1953. Countertransference and counteridentification. *Journal of the American Psychoanalytic Association* 1:268–284.

Freud, S. 1895. Studies on hysteria. *SE*, vol. 2. London: The Hogarth Press, 1964.

_____. 1910. The future prospects of psycho-analytic therapy. *SE*, vol. 11. London: The Hogarth Press, 1964.

_____. 1912. Recommendations to physicians practicing psychoanalysis. *SE*, vol. 12. London: The Hogarth Press, 1964.

_____. 1912. The dynamics of the transference. *SE*, vol. 12. London: The Hogarth Press, 1964.

_____. 1901. *Fragment of an Analysis of a Case of Hysteria. SE*, vol. 7. London: The Hogarth Press, 1964.

_____. 1914. Observations on transference-love. *SE*, vol. 12. London: The Hogarth Press, 1964.

_____. 1920. Beyond the pleasure principle. *SE*, vol. 18. London: The Hogarth Press, 1964.

_____. 1927–1931. Civilization and its discontents. *SE*, vol. 21. London: The Hogarth Press, 1964.

_____. 1937–1939. Constructions in analysis. *SE*, vol. 13. London: The Hogarth Press, 1964.

_____. 1985. *The Complete Letters of Sigmund Freud to Wilhelm Fliess*. Cambridge, Mass.: Harvard University Press.

Fuller, R. C. 1982. *Mesmerism and the American Cure of Souls*. Philadelphia: University of Pennsylvania Press.

Geymonat, L. 1985. *Lineamenti di filosofia della scienza*. Milan: Mondadori.

Giovacchini, P. L., ed. *Tactics and Techniques in Psychoanalytic Therapy, Vol. 2: Countertransference.* New York: Jason Aronson, Inc.

Goldberger, M., and Evans, D. 1985. On transference manifestations in male patients with female analysts. *International Journal of Psycho-Analysis* 66:295–309.

Gorkin, M. 1985. Varieties of sexualized countertransference. *Psychoanalytic Review* 72:421–440.

Green, M. 1976. *Else und Frieda, die Richtofen-Schwestern.* Monaco: Kindler.

Greenacre, P. 1954. The role of transference: practical considerations in relation to psychoanalytic therapy. *Journal of the American Psychoanalytic Association* 2:671–684.

Grünbaum, A. 1984. *The Foundations of Psychoanalysis.* Berkeley, Calif.: University of California Press.

Hempel, C. 1966. *Philosophy of Natural Science.* Englewood Cliffs, N.J.: Prentice-Hall.

Hillman, J. 1972. *The Myth of Analysis.* Evanston, Ill.: Northwestern University Press.

Hoffer, W. 1956. Transference and transference neurosis. *International Journal of Psycho-Analysis* 37:377–379.

Holmes, D. S. 1972. Repression or interference? A further investigation. *Journal of Personality and Social Psychology* 22:163–170.

Hunter, R., and Macalpine, I. 1971. *Three Hundred Years of Psychiatry 1535–1860.* London: Oxford University Press.

Jones, E. 1953. *Vita e opere di Freud*, vol. 1/3. Milan: Il Saggiatore, 1962. English translation, *The Life and Work of Sigmund Freud*, Lionel Trilling and Steven Marcus, eds. New York: Basic Books, 1961.

Jung, C. G. 1915. *Psychology of the Unconscious.* London: Kegan, Paul, Trench, Trubner, and Co, Ltd.

_____. 1934. The state of psychotherapy today. In *CW*, vol. 10. London: Routledge and Kegan Paul, 1964.

_____. 1938. Presidential address to the 10th International Medical Congress for Psychotherapy. In *CW*, vol. 10. London: Routledge and Kegan Paul, 1964.

_____. 1946. Psychology of the transference. In *CW*, vol. 16. London: Routledge and Kegan Paul, 1964. Also in *The Practice of Psychotherapy*. New York: Pantheon Books, Inc. 1954.

_____. 1960. Psychological factors determining human behavior. In *CW*, vol. 8. New York: Pantheon Books.

_____. 1961. *Memories, Dreams, Reflections*. New York: Pantheon Books.

_____. 1968. *Analytical Psychology*. London: Routledge and Kegan Paul.

Kant, I. 1787. *Critica della ragion pura [Critique of Pure Reason]*. Torino: Einaudi, 1957; New York: St. Martin's Press, 1968.

Kernberg, O. F. 1972. Psychotherapy and psychoanalysis. *Bulletin of the Menninger Clinic* 36.

Klein, M. 1957. *Envy and Gratitude*. Delacorte Press/Seymour Lawrence.

Kohut, H. 1971. *The Analysis of the Self*. London: The Hogarth Press.

Lakoff, G., and Johnson, M. 1980. *Metaphors We Live By*. Chicago: University of Chicago Press.

Laplanche, J., and Pontalis, J. B. 1967. *Enciclopedia della psicoanalisi*. Bari: Laterza, 1968. English translation, *The Language of Psycho-analysis*, Donald Nicholson-Smith, trans. New York: Norton, 1974.

Lester, E. P. 1985. The female analyst and the erotized transference. *International Journal of Psycho-Analysis* 66:283–294.

Lewin, K. 1935. *Teoria dinamica della personalità*. Firenze: Editrice Universitaria, 1965. English translation, *A Dynamic Theory of Personality*, Donald K. Adams, trans. New York: McGraw-Hill, 1935.

Liébeault, A. A. 1889. *Le sommeil provoqué et les états analogues*. New York: Arno Press, 1976.

Lorenz, C. 1963. *Il cosiddetto male*. Milan: Mondadori, 1969.

Maggiorani, C. 1880. *Influenza del magnetismo sulla vita animale*. Rome: Enrico Detken Editore.

Marks, R. W. 1947. *The Story of Hypnotism*. New York: Prentice-Hall.

Masson, J. M. 1984. *The Assault on Truth*. Toronto: Farrar, Strauss and Giroux.

McGuire, W., ed. 1974. *The Freud/Jung Letters*. London: Routledge and Kegan Paul.

Neumann, E. 1949. *Storia delle origini della conscienza.* Rome: Astrolabio, 1978. English translation, *The Origins and History of Consciousness.* New York: Pantheon Books, 1954.

———. 1955. Narcisismo, automorfismo e rapporto primario. *Rivista di Psicologia Analitica* 19:133–158.

———. 1959. The psychology of feminine development. *Spring.*

———. 1963. *The Child.* New York: Putnam's Sons, 1973.

Nietzsche, F. 1888/1889. *Frammenti postumi 1888–1889.* In *Opere di Friedrich Nietzsche*, vol. 8. Milan: Adelphi, 1974.

Ochberg, F. 1978. The victim of terrorism: psychiatric considerations. *Terrorism* 1.

Orr, D. W. 1954. Transference and countertransference: a historical survey. *Journal of the American Psychoanalytic Association* 2:621–670.

Paulet, J. J. 1784. *L'antimagnétisme ou origine, progrès, décadence, renouvellement et réfutation du magnétisme animal.* Paris: Editions Slatkine, 1980.

Pera, M., and Pitt, J. 1985. *I modi del progresso.* Milan: Il Saggiatore.

Podmore, F. 1963. *From Mesmer to Christian Science.* New York: University Books.

Poll, W. 1967. *Die Suggestion [Suggestion].* Munich: Kösel-Verlag.

Popper, K. 1963. *Conjectures and Refutations: The Growth of Scientific Knowledge.* New York: Basic Books.

Racker, H. 1968. *Transference and Countertransference.* London: The Hogarth Press.

Radiguet, R. 1924. *Il ballo del conte d'Orgel.* Milan: Mondadori, 1975. English translation, *The Count's Ball*, Malcolm Crowley, trans. New York: W. W. Norton, 1929.

Rausky, F. 1977. *Mesmer o la rivoluzione terapeutica.* Milan: Feltrinelli, 1980.

Rieff, P. 1959. *Freud: The Mind of the Moralist.* London: University Paperbacks.

Rondinone, A. 1985. *Studio sulla seduzione.* Unpublished manuscript. Corso di laurea in psicologia, Rome.

Schwartz-Salant, N. 1984. Archetypal factors underlying sexual acting-out in the transference-countertransference process. In *Transference/Countertransference*, Chiron Clinical Series. Wilmette, Ill.: Chiron Publications.

Searles, H. F. 1975. The patient as therapist to his analyst. In *Tactics and Techniques in Psychoanalytic Therapy*, Giovacchini, ed. New York: Jason Aronson, Inc.

Segal, H. 1964. *Introduction to the Work of Melanie Klein*. London: William Heinemann.

Servadio, E. 1938. *La ricerca psichica*. Rome: Paolo Cremonese.

Silverman, M. A. 1985. Countertransference and the myth of the perfectly analyzed analyst. *Psychoanalytic Quarterly* 54:175–199.

Smith, S. 1984. The sexually abused patient and the abusing therapist: a study in sadomasochistic relationships. *Psychoanalytic Psychology* 1:89–98.

––––––. 1985. The role of transference and countertransference in the sexual abuse of patients. Unpublished manuscript. California School of Professional Psychology.

Spielrein, S. 1912. Destruction as a cause of birth. *Giornale Storico di Psicologia Dimanica* 1(1977).

Spitz, R. A. 1958. Il primo anno di vita del bambino. Firenze: Giunti-Barbera, 1962. English translation, *The First Year of Life*. New York: International Universities Press, 1965.

Sterba, R. F. 1978. Discussioni di S. Freud. *Giornale Storico di Psicologia Dimanica* 8(1980).

Stern, A. 1924. On the counter-transference in psychoanalysis. *Psychoanalytic Review* 11:166–174.

Szasz, T. S. 1963. The concept of transference. *International Journal of Psycho-Analysis* 44:432–443.

Tauber, E. S. 1954. Exploring the therapeutic use of countertransference data. *Psychiatry* 17:331–336.

Taylor, C. 1982. Sexual intimacy between patient and analyst. *Quadrant* 15:47–54.

Tuomela, R. 1985. Scienza, protoscienza e pseudoscienza. In *I modi del progresso*, Pera and Pitt, eds. Milan: Il Saggiatore.

Ulanov, A. 1979. Follow-up treatment in cases of patient/therapist sex. *Journal of the American Academy of Psychoanalysis* 7:101–110.

Viederman, M. 1976. The influence of the person of the analyst on structural change: a case report. *Psychoanalytic Quarterly* 45:231–249.

Vinchon, J. 1971. *Il magnetismo animale. Mesmer e il suo segreto.* Rome: Astrolabio.

Watzlawick, P., Beavin, J. H., and Jackson, D. D. 1967. *Pragmatica della comunicazione umana.* Rome: Astrolabio, 1971. English translation, *Pragmatics of Human Communication.* New York: Norton, 1967.

Zweig, S. 1931. *L'anima che guarisce.* Milan: Sperling and Kupfer S. A., 1933.

Index

Breuer, ix, x-xi, xiv, 71–72, 74–75,
76, 78
Briquet, 49
Buber, M., 104

C

Cadaverine, 9–10
Cannibalism, 80
Cappellano, A., 42
Carotenuto, A., ix, xiv, xvi, 12, 13,
21, 39, 74, 86, 117, 129, 133,
134
Case examples, 17, 125–126,
127–129
Catalepsy, 49, 67
Catharsis, ix, xi, 74
Celine, L. F., 9
Charcot, J. M., 49, 61–62, 67, 72,
78
Charisma, 100, 113, 116, 125
Chertok, L., xix, 2, 26, 29, 40, 44,
84, 97, 105
"Chimney sweeping," xi
Christian God, 63, 115
Christian Science, 25
Christianity, 80, 101, 107, 115
Christian Church (*see* Christianity)
Cocaine, 73
Collective unconscious, 79
Communication, 53, 57–58, 136
empathic, 53–54
love as, 118
Count of Montecristo, The (Dumas),
26
Countertransference, ix, xi-xiii, xv-
xvi, xix, xxi, 35–36, 60, 72, 75, 78,
85, 87–88, 98–100, 104, 119, 123,
132, 134, 139
psychotic, xiv
Couple, relationship of (traditional),
24, 106
(*see also* love)
Creativity, 21–23, 39, 81, 135
artistic, 103
Cremerius, J., ix-xvi, xx, xxi
Crisis, 133

D

Dante, 42, 90, 126
De Amore (Cappellano), 42
Death drive, 97, 100–101
Death wish, 17–18, 21
De Broglie, L., 11
Defenses, 67–68, 77–78, 84, 91, 94,
104–105, 109, 118, 124–125
Dehing, J., 37
Deontology, 30–31
Depression, 48, 69
De Saussure, R., xvii, xix, 2, 7, 26,
29, 40, 97
Devil, 63–64, 89, 101, 133
De Villers, C., 2
Diary of a Secret Symmetry (Caro-
tenuto), 74
Didactic analysis, xi, 14–15, 88,
98–99, 115, 119–120, 129, 132
Dinnerstein, A., 57
Divinity, identification with, 14
relationship with, 107, 138
Dora, the analysis of, xvi, 97
Dreams, 79, 81, 125–126, 133,
134

E

Earth magnetism, 4
Edinger, E. F., 36
Education, 55, 57–58, 108, 119
Ego, 36, 39, 46, 66, 100, 125
Ego-Self axis, 36, 85, 102, 104, 135
Ehrenwald, J., 1, 2, 40
Eissler, K. R., xx, 91
Electroshock therapy, 71
Ellenberger, H. F., xviii, 2, 4, 5, 9,
25, 26, 29, 30, 40, 49, 61, 139
Emotion, 55–56, 68, 74–75, 76–78,
88, 92, 103, 110–111, 119,
121–123
artificial, 111
Emotional field, 98, 116
Emotional relationship, 110
Empathic relationship, 104
Envy, 19–23
Epistomology, 47, 72

Negation, 77, 86
Neumann, E., 6, 93
Neurology, 72, 76
Neurosis, 27, 39, 65, 90, 96,
    117–119 122, 129, 133
  etiology of, 83
  infantile, 58
  narcissistic, 96
  origins of, 20–21, 49, 52, 82
Nietzsche, 46
Night Porter (Cavani), 118

O

Object investment, 96–97
Object relationships, early, 100, 107,
  116
Objectification, 40, 43, 76–77, 93, 102
  of the therapeutic relationship, 41,
    47, 59, 63, 69–70, 74, 84, 89
Ochberg, F. M., 16
Oedipal stage (phase), 19, 54–55, 77,
    135, 140
Oedipus complex, xiv, 55, 137, 140
Ophthalmology, 73
Orr, D. W., 60

P

Paralysis, 49
  functional, 62–63
Paranoia, 63, 65
Paranormal faculties, 46–47
Parapsychology, 46
Patient/physician relationship, 67
Patient/therapist relationship, xviii,
    xxi, 4, 13, 18, 20, 51, 59, 70, 78,
    84, 89, 90, 125, 130
  asymmetry of, 13
  circular, 89
Patrimony, 93
  psychic, 125
Paulet, J. J., 2
Persona, 75, 77, 108
Personality, 108, 113
  of the magnetizer, 26
  of the therapist, 51, 90–91, 98–99,
    110, 115, 117

Pharmacology, 71
Phobia, 31, 65
Placebo effect, 27, 45, 71
Plato, 57, 114
Pleasure principle, 97
Podmore, F., 2, 26, 29, 40
Poe, E. A., 25
Poll, W., 52
Polygamy, xv
Pontalis, J. B., 97
Popper, K., 43
Positivism, 2, 18, 72, 74
Power, 11–14, 70, 88, 100, 113
Practice, of analysis, vs. theory, xix-
  xx
*Pragmatics in Human Communica-
  tion* (Watzlawich), 53
Primary object relationship, 86
Primary relationship, 6–7, 13, 54, 56,
    59, 75, 77, 86
Projection, 7–8, 13, 94, 100, 111,
    117, 137–138
Psychiatry
  classic, 71
  dynamic, 105
Psychic energy, 47–48, 87
Psychic infection, 104
Psychic phenomena, 33
  objectification of, 102
Psychic reality, 52, 83
Psychoanalysis, ix, xi-xii, xvi, xviii,
    78, 82–83, 98, 103
  and mesmerism, xix
  early years of, xiv, 116
  existential, 98, 118
  history of, xviii, 99
Psychoanalytic associations, admission
  to, 98
Psychodrama, 18
Psychological field, xviii, xix, xxi, 4,
    23, 97
Psychology of Transference, The
  (Jung), 90
Psychopathology, of the analyst, 85
Psychosomatic relationship, 44–45,
    48–49

Spiritism, 25

Spitz, R. A., 6

Sterba, R. F., 31

Stern, A., 35

Stockholm Syndrome, 16, 109, 118

Strindberg, xiv

Suggestion, in hypnosis, 45, 51–53, 72

Suicide, collective, 102

Superego, 100, 102

Symbols, 80–81

Symmetry, in analytic relationship, 33, 36

Symptom, 31–32, 64, 72, 74, 96, 108, 112

Syntony, 34, 35

Szasz, T. S., 84

T

Taboos, 65
  social, 114

"Talking cure," xi

Tao, 140

Tauber, E. S., 40, 99

Taylor, C., 129

Telepathy, 46

Tenderness, 28, 86, 126

Theophagy, 80

Theory, of analysis, 139–140
  versus practice, xix-xx, 10, 140

Therapeutic instrument, transference as, 1, 139

Therapeutic methods, xvii, 11

Therapeutic setting, 114–115, 119, 124, 127, 131, 136, 140–141

Therapeutic symbiosis, xxi

Transference, ix-xi, xiii-xv, xix, xxi, 1, 4–5, 20, 22, 35–36, 42, 60, 67, 72, 74–75, 78, 84, 87–88, 96–98, 100, 106–109, 111, 113, 119, 121, 123, 124, 126–127, 131, 134, 136–137, 139, 141
  early history of, 19, 76, 139
  objectified, 85

Transference love, xiii, xv, 60, 85, 104–105, 108–111, 113–115, 118

Transference neurosis, 96, 112, 115

Tub therapy, 5, 26

Tuomela, R., 1

U

Ulanov, A., 129

Unconscious, 35, 45–46, 52, 64, 79, 87, 98–99, 104, 108, 110, 120, 125, 131–132

Unifying theory, 47

Universal fluid, 3, 12

Uroboric relationship, 56–58, 67, 77, 86, 88, 92, 99

Uroboros, 6, 8, 135, 137

V

Viederman, M., 27

Vinchon, J., 2, 25

W

Watzlawich, P., 53

Wedeking, xiv

Will, 26
  to heal, 31–32, 71

Woman, xiv-xv

Y

Yoga, 45

Z

Zweig, S., 2